CONTENTS

INTRODUCTION

Christians in the world today hold the death and resurrection of Jesus as their only hope for salvation from sin and judgment and for their future hope of eternal life. The prophets of the Old Testament also grounded their hopes for redemption on Jesus, whom they knew as the promised Messiah. While believers today look back through faith to the salvation achieved by Christ, the Old Testament prophets looked forward through faith to the fulfillment of God's promised salvation. Perhaps no prophet looked forward with such detail and such beauty as Isaiah.

In these twelve studies, we will explore this book in all its history, prophecy, and laser-focus on the promises connected to the Messiah. We will learn about the prophet who spoke with power to both kings and commoners among God's people. We will hear of God's judgment pronounced against both the nation of Israel and her enemies. We will explore the promise of deliverance for Isaiah's contemporaries, and we will examine the wonderful descriptions of God's ultimate deliverance through the life and ministry of His suffering Servant, the Messiah.

Through it all, we will stay focused, as Isaiah did, on God's incredible promise of salvation for all who believe in Him and call Him their Lord.

TITLE

The book derives its title from the author, whose name in Hebrew means, "Yahweh [the LORD] is salvation." In this regard, *Isaiah* is similar to the names *Joshua*, *Elisha*, and *Jesus*, which carry the same meaning. The New Testament authors quoted passages from Isaiah more than sixty-five times—a greater number than any other other Old Testament prophet—and mentioned him by name more than twenty times (see, for example, Romans 9:29). In the Gospels, we read that Jesus began His ministry in Nazareth by quoting from the prophet Isaiah (see Luke 4:16–19).

AUTHOR AND DATE

Isaiah, the son of Amoz, ministered in and around Jerusalem as a prophet to Judah during the reigns of four kings of Judah: Uzziah (called "Azariah" in 2 Kings), Jotham, Ahaz, and Hezekiah (see Isaiah 1:1), from c. 739–686 BC. Isaiah was a contemporary of the prophets Hosea and Micah, and evidently came from a family of some rank, as he had easy access to the king (see 7:3). Isaiah was married and had two sons: Shear-jashub (meaning "a remnant shall return," see 7:3); and Maher-shalal-hash-baz (meaning "hastening to the spoil, hurrying to the prey," see 8:3). When God called Isaiah to prophesy in the year of King Uzziah's death, he responded with a cheerful readiness, even though he knew his ministry would be one of fruitless warning and exhortation (see 6:9–13). Having been raised in Jerusalem, he was an appropriate choice as a political and religious counselor to the nation. Isaiah the prophet lived until at least 681 BC, as he penned the account of Sennacherib's death (see 37:38). Tradition states he met his death under King Manasseh (c. 695–642 BC) by being cut in two with a wooden saw.

BACKGROUND AND SETTING

During Uzziah's prosperous fifty-two year reign (c. 790–739 BC), Judah developed into a strong commercial and military state, with a port for commerce on the Red Sea and many walled towers and fortifications (see 2 Chronicles 26:3–5, 8–10, 13–15). Yet the period also witnessed a decline in Judah's faithfulness to the Lord and spiritual purity. Uzziah's downfall resulted from his attempt to assume the privileges of a priest and burn incense on the altar (see 26:16–19). He was judged with leprosy, from which he never recovered (see 26:20–21).

Uzziah's son Jotham (c. 750–731 BC) took over the duties of king before his father's death. At the time, Assyria was emerging as an international power under Tiglath-Pileser (c. 745–727 BC), and the nation also began to incur opposition from Israel and Syria to the north (see 2 Kings 15:19, 37). Jotham was a builder and a fighter like his father, but spiritual corruption still existed in the land (see 2 Kings 15:34–35; 2 Chronicles 27:1–2).

ISAIAH

The Promise of the Messiah

John MacArthur

THOMAS NELSON
Since 1798

MacArthur Bible Studies
Isaiah: The Promise of the Messiah
© 2020 by John MacArthur

Published in Nashville, Tennessee, by Thomas Nelson. Thomas Nelson is a registered trademark of HarperCollins Christian Publishing, Inc.

"Unleashing God's Truth, One Verse at a Time ®" is a trademark of Grace to You. All rights reserved.

All Scripture quotations are taken from The Holy Bible, New King James Version. Copyright © 1979, 1980, 1982 by Thomas Nelson. All rights reserved.

Some material from the Introduction, "Keys to the Text" and "Exploring the Meaning" sections are taken from *The MacArthur Bible Commentary*, John MacArthur. Copyright © 2005 Thomas Nelson Publishers.

Thomas Nelson titles may be purchased in bulk for educational, business, fundraising, or sales promotional use. For information, please e-mail SpecialMarkets@ThomasNelson.com.

ISBN 978-0-310-12380-4 (softcover)
ISBN 978-0-310-12381-1 (ebook)

First Printing November 2020 / Printed in the United States of America

Jotham's son Ahaz (c. 735–715 BC) ruled from age twenty-five to forty-one (see 2 Chronicles 28:1, 8). During his reign, Israel and Syria formed an alliance to combat the rising Assyrian threat, but Ahaz refused to bring Judah into it (see 2 Kings 16:5). As a result, his northern neighbors threatened to dethrone him, and war resulted. In a panic, Ahaz solicited the Assyrian king for help (see 2 Kings 16:7). The Assyrian king gladly responded, sacking Gaza, carrying Galilee and Gilead into captivity, and capturing Damascus (c 732 BC). Ahaz's alliance with Assyria led to his introduction of a pagan altar, which he set up in Solomon's temple. In 722 BC, Assyria captured Samaria, capital of the northern kingdom, and carried many of Israel's most capable people into captivity (see 2 Kings 17:6, 24).

Ahaz's son Hezekiah (c. 716–686 BC) made spiritual reformation a priority when he assumed the throne (see 2 Kings 18:1–2, 4, 22). By this point, the threat of an Assyrian invasion had forced Judah to promise heavy tribute to that eastern power. In 701 BC, Hezekiah became ill with a life-threatening disease, but God graciously extended his life by fifteen years (see 20:1–11). The ruler of Babylon used the opportunity of Hezekiah's illness and recovery to send congratulations to him, likely hoping to form an alliance with Judah against Assyria (see 20:12).

When Assyria became weak through internal strife, Hezekiah refused to pay any further tribute to that power (see 18:7). As a result, the Assyrian king Sennacherib invaded the coastal areas of Israel, marching toward Egypt on Israel's southern flank. In the process, he overran Judean towns, looting and carrying many people back to Assyria. While besieging Lachish, he sent a contingent to surround Jerusalem (see 18:17–19:8). When this side expedition failed, he sent messengers to Jerusalem, demanding immediate surrender (see 19:9). With Isaiah's encouragement, Hezekiah refused to surrender (see Isaiah 37:1–7). Sennacherib's army fell prey to a sudden disaster, and he returned to Nineveh and never threatened Judah again.

HISTORICAL AND THEOLOGICAL THEMES

Isaiah prophesied during the period of the divided kingdom, though he directed most of his prophecies to the southern kingdom of Judah. He condemned the empty ritualism of his day and the idolatry into which the people had fallen (see Isaiah 1:10–15; 40:18–20). He foresaw the coming Babylonian captivity because of Judah's departure from the Lord (see 39:6–7).

Some of Isaiah's prophecies were fulfilled during his lifetime, which provided his credentials for the prophetic office. For instance, Sennacherib's effort to take Jerusalem failed, just as Isaiah had said it would (see 37:6–7, 36–38). God healed Hezekiah's critical illness, as Isaiah had predicted (see 38:5). Long before Cyrus, king of Persia, appeared on the scene, Isaiah named him as Judah's deliverer from the Babylonian captivity (see 44:28; 45:1). Fulfillment of his prophecies concerning Christ's first coming have given Isaiah further vindication (see, for example, 7:14). The literal fulfillment pattern of his already-fulfilled prophecies gives assurance that prophecies of Christ's second coming will also see literal fulfillment.

Isaiah provides information on the future Day of the Lord and the time that will follow (see, for example, Isaiah 2:12–21). He details numerous aspects of Israel's future kingdom on earth that are not found elsewhere in Scripture. These details include changes in nature and the animal world, Jerusalem's status among the nations, and the Suffering Servant's leadership.

Isaiah employed a literary device called "prophetic foreshortening" to predict future events without delineating exact sequences of the events or time intervals separating them. For example, nothing in Isaiah reveals the extended period separating the two comings of the Messiah (see Isaiah 61:1–2; Luke 4:17–22). Also, Isaiah does not provide as clear a distinction between the future temporal kingdom and the eternal kingdom, as John does in Revelation (see 20:1–10; 21:1–22:5). In God's program of progressive revelation, the details of these relationships awaited a prophetic spokesman in a later time.

Isaiah, also known as the "evangelical prophet," spoke much about the grace of God toward Israel, particularly in his last twenty-seven chapters. The centerpiece of his book is found in Isaiah 53, in which he portrays Christ as the slain Lamb of God. As Isaiah writes, "But He was wounded for our transgressions, He was bruised for our iniquities; the chastisement for our peace was upon Him, and by His stripes we are healed" (verse 5).

INTERPRETIVE CHALLENGES

Interpretive challenges in a long and significant book such as Isaiah are numerous. The most critical of them focuses on whether Isaiah's prophecies will receive literal fulfillment or not and on whether the Lord, in His program of the ages, has abandoned national Israel and permanently replaced the nation with the church, so that there is no future for national Israel.

On the latter issue, numerous portions of Isaiah support the position that God has not replaced ethnic Israel with an alleged "new Israel." Isaiah has too much to say about God's faithfulness to Israel—that He would not reject the people whom He has created and chosen (see 43:1). The nation is on the palms of His hands, and Jerusalem's walls are ever before His eyes (see 49:16). He is bound by His own Word to fulfill the promises He has made to bring them back to Himself and bless them in that future day (see 55:10–12).

On the former issue, literal fulfillment of many of Isaiah's prophecies has already occurred, so it is biblically groundless to contend that those yet unfulfilled will not see literal fulfillment. This fact also disqualifies the case for proposing that the church will receive many of the promises made originally to Israel. The kingdom promised to David belongs to Israel, not the church. The future exaltation of Jerusalem will be on earth, not in heaven. Christ will reign on this present earth, as well as in the future new heavens and new earth (see Revelation 22:1, 3).

JUDAH'S SOCIAL SINS

Isaiah 1:1–2:22; 5:1–6:13

DRAWING NEAR

How do you typically respond when you face tragedy or loss?

_____

_____

_____

_____

_____

_____

_____

_____

THE CONTEXT

The nation of Israel reached its peak under the leadership of King David and King Solomon (c. 1005 BC–928 BC). During that time, Israel expanded its territory, wealth, and influence in the region. Tragically, the nation was split in two when Solomon's son, Rehoboam, failed to demonstrate the wisdom of his father (see 1 Kings 12). The result was two nations: the northern kingdom, which retained the name Israel, and the southern kingdom of Judah.

The centuries following this split were marked by serious decline, both politically and spiritually, for each kingdom. The nation of Israel was continually led by a succession of evil kings, who actively pushed God's people into idolatry. As a result, Israel was eventually conquered in 722 BC by the rising nation of Assyria, and its people were dispersed. Judah, the southern kingdom, endured a mix of righteous and unrighteous leaders, yet eventually succumbed to a similar fate. Babylon conquered Judah and destroyed Jerusalem in 586 BC, taking the best and brightest of its citizens into captivity.

The failure of each kingdom's political and spiritual leaders during this time gave rise to the prophets. This collection of individuals was called specifically by God to declare His Word to His people. The prophets proclaimed a variety of messages, including words of warning and judgment, which often made them unpopular in their time.

Isaiah's prophetic ministry was mostly confined to the southern kingdom of Judah. He began his work after the death of Uzziah, who had reigned as Judah's king for more than fifty years. Isaiah ultimately spoke on God's behalf in the presence of four kings: Jotham, Ahaz, Hezekiah, and Manasseh. As you will see in this lesson, his work began with a stunning condemnation of Judah's sinfulness as a society and a proclamation of future judgment.

KEYS TO THE TEXT

Read Isaiah 1:1–2:22, noting the key words and phrases indicated below.

> *A COURTROOM SCENE: The book of Isaiah begins with a courtroom scene in which the Lord is the plaintiff and the nation of Israel is the defendant.*

1:2. HEAR, O HEAVENS . . . O EARTH: God intended Israel to be a channel of blessing to the nations (see Genesis 12:2–3), but now He must call the nations to look on Israel's shame. God declares that His "children," the physical descendants of Abraham, have rebelled against Him.

3. THE OX . . . THE DONKEY: Animals appear to have more powers of reason than God's people who break fellowship with Him.

4. THE HOLY ONE OF ISRAEL: Isaiah's special title for God, found twenty-five times in this book, but only six times in the rest of the Old Testament. Isaiah also uses "Holy One" as a title four times (see 10:17; 40:25; 43:15; 49:7) and "Holy One of Jacob" once (see 29:23). In many contexts, the name contrasts the holiness of God with the sinfulness of Israel.

5. WHY SHOULD YOU BE STRICKEN AGAIN?: The nation of Judah, already in ruins because of their rebellion against God, was behaving irrationally by continuing their rebellion.

8. DAUGHTER OF ZION: This phrase occurs twenty-eight times in the Old Testament, six of which are found in Isaiah (see 1:8; 10:32; 16:1; 37:22; 52:2; 62:11). The phrase is a personification of Jerusalem, and here stands for all of Judah.

9. LORD OF HOSTS: Isaiah used this title, or the similar "LORD God of hosts," sixty times. It pictures God as a mighty warrior, a leader of armies, who is capable of conquering all of Israel's enemies and providing for her survival.

REMNANT: Sometimes rendered "survivors," this term designates the faithful among the Israelites. Paul later cited this verse to prove the ongoing existence of faithful Israelites, even in his day (see Romans 9:29). Such a remnant will constitute the nucleus of returning Israelites in the nation's regathering when the Messiah returns to earth.

> SODOM AND GOMORRAH: *The prophet applies the names of the sinful cities to Judah and Jerusalem, decrying their empty formalism in worship.*

10. RULERS OF SODOM . . . PEOPLE OF GOMORRAH: God rained brimstone and fire on these two Canaanite cities because of their aggravated sinfulness (see Genesis 18:20; 19:24–28). The two cities later became a proverbial expression for the ultimate in God's temporal judgment against any people (see, for example, Jeremiah 23:14; 49:18; 50:40; Matthew 10:15; 2 Peter 2:6). Had God's grace not intervened, He would have judged Israel in the same way.

11. I HAVE HAD ENOUGH . . . I DO NOT DELIGHT: God found all sacrifices meaningless and even abhorrent if the offerer failed in obedience to His laws (see 1 Samuel 15:22–23). Rebellion is equated to the sin of witchcraft and stubbornness to iniquity and idolatry.

13–14. NEW MOONS, THE SABBATHS . . . ASSEMBLIES . . . APPOINTED FEASTS: These were all occasions prescribed by the law of Moses (see Exodus 12:16; Leviticus 23; Numbers 10:10; 28:11–29:40; Deuteronomy 16:1–17).

14. MY SOUL HATES: It is impossible to doubt the Lord's total aversion toward hypocritical religion. Other practices God hates include robbery for burnt offering (see 61:8), serving other gods (see Jeremiah 44:4), harboring evil against a neighbor and love for a false oath (see Zechariah 8:16), divorce (see Malachi 2:16), and those who love violence (see Psalm 11:5).

3

16. PUT AWAY THE EVIL: The outward evidence of the emptiness of Jerusalem's ritualism was the presence of evil works and the absence of good works.

17. THE FATHERLESS . . . THE WIDOW: Illustrative of good works and deeds done on behalf of those in need. "Pure and undefiled religion before God and the Father is this: to visit orphans and widows in their trouble, and to keep oneself unspotted from the world" (James 1:27).

18. SCARLET . . . CRIMSON: These colors speak of the guilt of those whose hands were "full of blood" (verse 15). Fullness of blood speaks of extreme iniquity and perversity.

WHITE AS SNOW . . . AS WOOL: Snow and wool are substances that are naturally white and, therefore, portray what is clean—the blood-guilt having been removed. In this way, the Lord promises to pardon and cleanse those whom He saves. (This section previews the last twenty-seven chapters of Isaiah, which focus more on God's grace and forgiveness than on judgment.)

19. WILLING AND OBEDIENT: While Isaiah is a prophet of grace, forgiveness is not unconditional. It comes through repentance. In this regard, the prophet offers his readers the same choice that God gave Moses in Deuteronomy 28: a choice between a blessing and a curse. They may choose repentance and obedience in order to reap the benefits of the land, or they can refuse to do so and become victims of foreign oppressors.

19–20. EAT . . . BE DEVOURED: God uses the same Hebrew word in these verses to accentuate opposite outcomes. On the one hand, the people can choose to eat the fruit of the land. On the other hand, they can choose to be eaten by conquering powers.

THE DEGENERATE CITY: These verses recount Jerusalem's disobedience, with an account of God's future actions to purge her of sin.

21. A HARLOT: In the Old Testament, spiritual harlotry was often used to depict the idolatry of God's people. However, in this instance, Jerusalem's unfaithfulness incorporates a wider range of wrongs, including murders and general corruption. As Isaiah prophesies, ethical depravity has replaced the city's former virtues.

24. THE LORD . . . THE LORD OF HOSTS, THE MIGHTY ONE OF ISRAEL: This threefold title of God emphasizes His role as the rightful Judge of His sinful

people. "The Mighty One of Israel" occurs only here in the Bible, though "the Mighty One of Jacob" appears five times (see Isaiah 49:26; 60:16; Genesis 49:24; Psalm 132:2, 5).

26. I WILL RESTORE: God's judgment of His people has future restoration as its goal. Ultimately, the people were restored from Babylonian captivity, but this promise has in view a greater and more lasting restoration. It anticipates a complete and permanent restoration, which will make Jerusalem supreme among the nations.

27. ZION: Originally a designation for the hill Ophel, this name became a synonym for the entire city of Jerusalem. Isaiah always uses it this way. The remnant of this city who repent of their sin will find redemption in conjunction with God's future restoration of Israel's prosperity.

28. TRANSGRESSORS . . . SINNERS: Concurrent with the future blessing of the faithful remnant, God will relegate the unrepentant to destruction. This is the only way Zion can become pure.

29. TEREBINTH TREES . . . GARDENS: These were settings where Israel practiced idolatrous worship. God had chosen Israel, but some of its people had chosen the gardens. When God calls them to account for their rebellious choice, they will be ashamed and embarrassed.

31. WILL BURN . . . NO ONE SHALL QUENCH: Both the rebellious and their works will perish. This is final judgment, not merely another captivity.

THE FUTURE HOUSE OF GOD: The prophet Isaiah provides a picture of Zion (or Jerusalem) as a "house of God" to depict her future exaltation.

2:2. IT SHALL COME TO PASS: The prophet Micah includes this portion of Isaiah's prophecy in his book almost word for word (see Micah 4:1–3), which indicates that this younger contemporary might have obtained the words from Isaiah. Both passages present a prophetic picture of Zion in the future, messianic kingdom when all people will recognize Jerusalem as the capital of the world.

2. IN THE LATTER DAYS: The latter (or last) days is a time designation that looks forward to the messianic era (see Ezekiel 38:16; Hosea 3:5; Micah 4:1). The authors of the New Testament applied the expression to the period beginning with the First Advent of Christ (see Acts 2:17; 2 Timothy 3:1; Hebrews 1:2).

Old Testament prophets, being without a clear word regarding the time between the Messiah's two advents, linked the expression to the Messiah's return to establish His earthly kingdom (that is, the millennial kingdom spoken of in Revelation 20:1–10).

3. THE MOUNTAIN OF THE LORD'S HOUSE: Mount Zion, the location of the temple in Jerusalem. The expression occurs two other times in the Old Testament (see 2 Chronicles 33:15; Micah 4:1). Isaiah frequently calls Mount Zion the "holy mountain" (see, for example, 11:9; 27:13; 56:7).

4. SWORDS INTO PLOWSHARES ... SPEARS INTO PRUNING HOOKS: With the Messiah on His throne in Jerusalem, the world will enjoy uninterrupted peaceful conditions. Warfare will continue to characterize human history until the Prince of Peace returns to earth to put an end to it.

> ANOTHER REBUKE: *After providing this glimpse of Judah's glorious future, the prophet returns to the present, offering a scathing rebuke of the people's idolatry and the judgment of God it will evoke.*

6. THEY ARE FILLED WITH EASTERN WAYS: An influx of religious superstitions had filled Jerusalem and its environs through caravans from the East. In this manner, through verse 9, Isaiah states the Lord's formal charge against the people of Jerusalem.

8. FULL OF IDOLS: Jotham and Ahaz, two of the kings under whom Isaiah prophesied, had failed to remove the idolatrous high places from the land (see 2 Kings 15:35; 16:4).

10–22. ENTER INTO THE ROCK: This section pictures conditions during the future Day of the Lord. While some elements fit what Judah experienced during the Babylonian captivity, the intensity of judgment predicted here could not have found fulfillment at that time. The Tribulation period before Christ's return will be the time for these judgmental horrors.

12. THE DAY OF THE LORD: This phrase appears nineteen times in the Old Testament and four times in the New Testament to express the time of God's extreme wrath. It can refer to a *near* future judgment or to a *far* future judgment. At times, the near fulfillment prefigures the far fulfillment (see Joel 1:15; 3:14); on other occasions, both kinds of fulfillment are included in one passage (see Zephaniah 1:7, 14). Here, Isaiah looks to the far fulfillment at the end of the time

of Jacob's trouble (see Jeremiah 30:7). Two "Day of the Lord" expressions remain to be fulfilled: (1) at the end of Daniel's seventieth week (see Joel 3:14; Malachi 4:5; 1 Thessalonians 5:2); and (2) at the end of the Millennium (see 2 Peter 3:10).

13. CEDARS OF LEBANON . . . OAKS OF BASHAN: The cedars and oaks were objects of great admiration to people in Old Testament times. Yet even these impressive created objects will face destruction because of human rebellion.

19. HOLES OF THE ROCKS . . . CAVES OF THE EARTH: John uses this passage (and verse 21) to describe humanity's flight from the terrors of Tribulation during the period before Christ's return to earth (see Revelation 6:12, 15–16). This reveals that the final fulfillment of this prophecy will be during Daniel's seventieth week.

22. SEVER YOURSELVES: This calls readers to stop depending on other humans and to trust only in God, who alone is worthy.

Read Isaiah 5:1–6:13, noting the key words and phrases indicated below.

A DISAPPOINTING VINEYARD: The conclusion of the prophet's extended discourse (first begun in Isaiah 2:1) comes by way of a comparison of God's people to a vineyard that He cultivated but which did not bear fruit.

1. MY WELL-BELOVED: The Lord is the friend who is well-beloved by Isaiah. The vineyard belongs to Him.

2. GOOD GRAPES . . . WILD GRAPES: The owner made every conceivable provision for the vine's productivity and protection, illustrating the Lord's purely gracious choice of Israel. Justifiably, He expected a good yield from His investment, but the vine's produce was "sour berries," inedible and fit only for dumping.

5. IT SHALL BE BURNED . . . TRAMPLED DOWN: As punishment for her unfruitfulness, Israel would become desolate and accessible to any nation wishing to invade her. This happened in the Babylonian invasion of 586 BC, and it will happen repeatedly until her national repentance at the second coming of the Messiah.

8. WOE TO THOSE WHO JOIN HOUSE TO HOUSE: The prophet will now (through verse 23) pronounce six woes or judgments against the unresponsive

people of Israel. The first woe is against real estate owners because of their greedy materialism. God gave the land to the Israelites with the intention that the original allocation remain with each family. By Isaiah's time, land speculators were putting together huge estates, and the powerful rich were using legal processes to deprive the poor of what was rightfully theirs.

10. ONE BATH . . . ONE EPHAH: God judged the greedy rich by reducing the productivity of their land to a small fraction of what it would have been normally. One bath was roughly equivalent to six gallons. About onehalf bushel would be produced from about six bushels of planted seed. Such amounts indicate famine conditions.

11. Woe to those who rise . . . that they may follow intoxicating drink: The second woe addresses the drunkards for their neglect of the Lord's work of judgment and redemption, and for their devotion to pleasure.

14. SHEOL: This term, in this context, pictures death as a great monster with wide-open jaws, ready to receive its victims. Such is to be the fate of those who perish in the captivity that God will send to punish the people's sinfulness.

18. WOE TO THOSE WHO DRAW INIQUITY WITH CORDS OF VANITY: The third woe is against those who defied the Lord and ridiculed His prophet.

19. LET HIM MAKE SPEED: The taunting unbelievers said, in effect, "Where is the judgment of which you have spoken? We will believe it when we see it." This challenge for God to hasten His judgment represents their disbelief that the Holy One of Israel will judge the people.

20. WOE TO THOSE WHO CALL EVIL GOOD, AND GOOD EVIL: The fourth woe condemns the reversal of morality that dominated the nation. They utterly confused all moral distinctions.

21. WOE TO THOSE WHO ARE WISE IN THEIR OWN EYES: The object of the fifth woe relates to the people's arrogance. "Pride goes before destruction" (Proverbs 16:18).

22–23. WOE TO MEN . . . WHO JUSTIFY THE WICKED: The sixth woe points to the unjust sentences passed by drunken and bribed judges.

26. NATIONS FROM AFAR: The conclusion of the discourse announces God's action in sending a mighty army against Judah to conquer and leave the land in darkness and distress. Principal among these nations were Assyria, which conquered the northern kingdom in 722 BC, and Babylon, which completed its invasion of Jerusalem in 586 BC and destroyed the temple.

30. DARKNESS AND SORROW: God's wrath against the people was intended to eliminate light (see Isaiah 8:22; 42:7), but His promised deliverance of the remnant will ultimately turn that darkness into light at the coming of the Messiah (see 9:2; 42:16; 58:10; 60:2).

ISAIAH'S CALL: The Lord, in calling Isaiah to be the prophet who would proclaim the coming judgment, gave him a vision of His majestic holiness so overwhelming that it devastated Isaiah and made him realize his own sinfulness.

6:1. KING UZZIAH DIED: After fifty-two years of rule, Uzziah succumbed to leprosy in 739 BC. Isaiah began his prophetic ministry that same year. He received the prophecies recounted in Isaiah 1–5 after this call, but here he returns to authenticate what he has already written by describing how he was called.

I SAW THE LORD . . . HIGH AND LIFTED UP: The prophet Isaiah became unconscious of the outside world and, with his inner eye, saw what God revealed to him. The throne he saw was greatly elevated, emphasizing the Most High God. This experience recalls the experience of John's prophetic vision in Revelation 4:1–11.

TRAIN: This refers to the hem or fringe of the Lord's robe that filled the temple.

TEMPLE: Isaiah may have been at the earthly temple, but this vision transcends the earthly. The throne of God is in the heavenly temple (see Revelation 4:1–6; 5:1–7; 11:19).

2. SERAPHIM: The seraphim are an order of angelic creatures who bear a similarity to the four living creatures of Revelation 4:6, which in turn resemble the cherubim of Ezekiel 10:1.

SIX WINGS: Two wings covered the faces of the seraphim because they dared not gaze directly at God's glory. Two covered their feet, acknowledging their lowliness, even though engaged in divine service. With two, they flew in serving the One on the throne. Thus, the four wings relate to worship, emphasizing the priority of praise.

3. ONE CRIED TO ANOTHER: The seraphim were speaking to each other in antiphonal praise.

HOLY, HOLY, HOLY: The primary thrust of this threefold repetition of God's holiness (called the *trihagion*) emphasizes God's separateness from and independence of His fallen creation, though it implies secondarily that God is three persons.

FULL OF HIS GLORY: The earth is the worldwide display case for God's immeasurable glory, perfections, and attributes as seen in creation. Fallen man has nevertheless refused to glorify Him as God (see Romans 1:20, 23).

4. SHAKEN . . . SMOKE: This symbolizes God's holiness as it relates to His wrath and judgment (see Exodus 19:16–20; Revelation 15:8).

5. UNCLEAN LIPS: If the lips are unclean, so is the heart. This vision of God's holiness vividly reminded the prophet of his own unworthiness, which deserved judgment. Job and Peter came to the same realization when confronted with God's presence (see Job 42:6; Luke 5:8).

6. COAL . . . ALTAR: The hot coal taken from the altar of incense in heaven is emblematic of God's purifying work (see Revelation 8:3–5). Repentance is painful, and this vision has made Isaiah painfully aware of his own sin. In this way, God has prepared him for his commission.

7. TAKEN AWAY . . . PURGED: Spiritual cleansing for special service to the Lord, not salvation, is in view here.

8. US: This plural pronoun does not explicitly prove the doctrine of the Trinity, but it does strongly imply it (see Genesis 1:26).

HERE AM I! SEND ME: This response from Isaiah reveals his humble readiness and complete trust in God. Though he was profoundly aware of his sin, he was available.

9. DO NOT UNDERSTAND . . . DO NOT PERCEIVE: Isaiah's message was to be God's instrument for hiding the truth from an unreceptive people. Centuries later, Jesus' parables were to do the same (see Matthew 13:14–15; Mark 4:12; Luke 8:10).

11. HOW LONG?: The prophet Isaiah, knowing the people's rejection of the Lord, asks how long he should preach this message of divine judgment. God replies that it must continue until the cities are desolate and the people have gone into exile.

13. A TENTH: Though most will reject God, the tenth (also called "stumps" and "holy seed") represents the faithful remnant in Israel who will be the nucleus who hear and believe.

UNLEASHING THE TEXT

1) How would you describe the overall tone of Isaiah's prophecy in these opening chapters?

_____

_____

_____

_____

_____

2) What are some of Judah's specific sins that caught your attention? Why?

_____

_____

_____

_____

3) What are some of the judgments or punishments described in these opening chapters?

_____

_____

_____

_____

_____

4) What can you learn about God from Isaiah's call to be a prophet in chapter 6?

_____

_____

_____

_____

_____

EXPLORING THE MEANING

God is our righteous Judge. The action in Isaiah takes off right at the start. In Isaiah 1:2, the prophet proclaims, "Hear, O heavens, and give ear, O earth! For the LORD has spoken: 'I have nourished and brought up children, and they have rebelled against Me.'" He goes on in the remainder of the chapter to list the ways that God's people have fallen short of His standards.

In opening his book this way, Isaiah quickly and clearly displays God's authority not only over the people of Judah but also over the entire world. ("Hear, O *heavens*, and give ear, O *earth!*") The people of Isaiah's day believed they retained a degree of autonomy over their everyday lives. They acknowledged God's existence and even worshiped Him through sacrifice, yet they chose to live in habitual disobedience to His will. Isaiah's immediate focus on God as the righteous Judge over all the earth is a reminder that He has both the power and the authority to stand in judgment over humanity. He knows all things and is well able to provide correction when people reject Him—both on the individual and the national level.

Even so, God reveals His love for His people by highlighting the possibility of forgiveness: "'Come now, and let us reason together,' says the LORD, 'Though your sins are like scarlet, they shall be as white as snow; though they are red like crimson, they shall be as wool'" (verse 18). Like so much of Isaiah's prophecy to the people of Judah, these verses point forward to the coming salvation purchased by the death and resurrection of Jesus.

God will one day fully execute His authority as Judge. God is both just and merciful, which means He is patient and loving with His people even as He punishes their sin. Throughout the Old Testament, God interacted with the Israelites in much the same way that parents show love and discipline to their children. Namely, God exhibited an extreme amount of patience in the face of rejection and rebellion. After all, He wanted His people to turn back to Him. When He did bring judgment, such as the destruction of Jerusalem at the hands of the Babylonians, His actions always pointed ahead to future grace and restoration.

However, there will come a time when God's full wrath against sin will be revealed. In Scripture, this is often called "the Day of the Lord," and it refers to the end of history when God will fully root out the corruption of evil and sin from His creation. Isaiah refers to this coming day several times in his prophecies, including in Isaiah 2: "For the day of the LORD of hosts shall come upon everything proud and lofty, upon everything lifted up—and it shall be brought low. . . . The loftiness of man shall be bowed down, and the haughtiness of men shall be brought low; the LORD alone will be exalted in that day" (verses 12, 17).

The language Isaiah uses to describe that day is both striking and terrifying. "They shall go into the holes of the rocks, and into the caves of the earth," he writes, "from the terror of the LORD and the glory of His majesty, when He arises to shake the earth mightily" (verse 19). He describes people running "from the terror of the Lord" and God arising "to shake the earth mightily" (verses 21–22). In short, the Day of the Lord will be a time of judgment unlike anything ever seen. Yet for God's people, it will also lead to a time of rejoicing, because God will finally remove the stain and corruption of sin once and for all.

Serving God is an awesome responsibility. In Isaiah 6, the prophet recalls the moment when God appeared to him in a vision called him into His service. "I heard the voice of the Lord, saying: 'Whom shall I send, and who will go for Us?'" Many readers of the Bible are inspired by Isaiah's quick response: "Here am I! Send me'" (verse 8).

However, it's important not to miss Isaiah's earlier interaction with God at the beginning of the chapter. After the death of King Uzziah, Isaiah supernaturally witnessed a vision of God's heavenly throne room. The sight was both awesome and terrible, causing Isaiah to cry out, "Woe is me, for I am undone! Because I am a man of unclean lips, and I dwell in the midst of a people of unclean lips; for my eyes have seen the King, the LORD of hosts" (verse 5).

Isaiah's cry mirrors Peter's after he recognized Jesus as the Messiah and exclaimed, "Depart from me, for I am a sinful man, O Lord!" (Luke 5:8). In fact, throughout the Bible, people almost unanimously fall to the ground and worship in fear whenever they come into God's presence. Those of us who serve as disciples of Jesus today will do well to remember that our Savior is also the supreme Lord and Judge of the universe. Our service to Him is not a casual commitment but rather an awesome responsibility.

REFLECTING ON THE TEXT

5) How do you typically respond to passages about judgment and punishment in the Bible? Why do you respond that way?

----

6) Why does Scripture include the terrible imagery connected with "the Day of the Lord"?

_____

_____

_____

_____

7) When confronted with the greatness of God, have you ever felt a sense of fear or wonder? Explain.

_____

_____

_____

_____

8) What is the proper way to understand God's mercy balanced with His justice? How can you reconcile the apparent tension between those two?

_____

_____

_____

_____

PERSONAL RESPONSE

9) What steps can you take this week to reflect on God's presence and worship Him?

_____

_____

_____

_____

10) Where do you currently have an opportunity to tell someone about the reality of God's future judgment?

_____

_____

_____

_____

2

JUDAH'S POLITICAL ENTANGLEMENTS
Isaiah 7:1–25; 9:1–11:16

DRAWING NEAR
How do you typically handle telling someone bad news?

_____

_____

_____

_____

_____

_____

_____

_____

_____

_____

THE CONTEXT
In the previous lesson, we were introduced to Isaiah the prophet. As we discussed, he was a man called by God who ministered to both the kings and the common people of Judah for decades. The first five chapters of Isaiah's book focused on the consequences of Judah's social sins, and particularly the empty ritualism of their religious observances. In Isaiah 6, the prophet recounted his original call, which both devastated and inspired him.

The next section of Isaiah's prophecy begins with an imminent historical crisis. Rezin, the king of Syria, and Pekah, the king of Israel (the northern kingdom), had brought their armies to the outskirts of Jerusalem to "make war" against Judah (7:1). In addition, the nation of Assyria had risen as a danger-ous threat in the region. This was a time of fear for the people of Judah, es-pecially those living in Jerusalem. In response, God sent Isaiah to reveal what was about to happen—specifically, that the residents of Jerusalem would be spared destruction.

This was good news for the people of Judah. Furthermore, to encourage King Ahaz, the Lord offered to send him a sign. But the king, in false humility, refused—to which God declared that He would choose His own sign. And as we will see in this lesson, this sign would represent God's plan of salvation for more than just the immediate threat facing Judah. In fact, it would repre-sent His ultimate plan of salvation for all of humanity.

Keys to the Text

Read Isaiah 7:1–25, noting the key words and phrases indicated below.

> *A Prophecy to the King: Isaiah declared God's Word to Ahaz, king of Judah, speaking promises of both judgment and deliverance.*

7:1. IT CAME TO PASS: An unsuccessful invasion of Judah by Syria and Israel (the ten northern tribes) led to the continued presence of King Tiglath-Pileser's Assyrian forces in Israel. Shortly after Ahaz assumed the throne (c. 735 BC), this threat to Judah's security brought great fear to the king and the people of Judah (see 2 Chronicles 28:5–8, 17–19).

2. HOUSE OF DAVID: This expression refers to the Davidic dynasty, personified in the current king, Ahaz.

3. SHEAR-JASHUB: The name means "a remnant shall return." The pres-ence of Isaiah's son is an object lesson of God's faithfulness to believers among the people.

4. DO NOT FEAR: Isaiah's message to Ahaz is one of reassurance. The two invading kings would not prevail against Judah.

8. EPHRAIM WILL BE BROKEN: This tribe represented the ten northern tribes. The prophet predicted the coming demise because of idolatry. In sixty-five years they would cease to be a people, first through captivity in 722 BC (see 2 Kings 17:6), and then through the importation of foreign settlers into the land in 670 BC (see 2 Kings 17:24).

9. IF YOU WILL NOT BELIEVE . . . NOT BE ESTABLISHED: The choice belonged to Ahaz. He could trust the Lord's word or fall into the enemy's hands or, even worse, experience a final hardening of his heart.

> A SIGN FROM GOD: *The Lord offers to provide a sign of Ahaz's own choosing, to show that His word is true. When Ahaz refuses, God declares that He will send His own sign—the fulfillment of which would not take place until the birth of Jesus, the promised Messiah.*

11–12. ASK A SIGN: To encourage Ahaz's faith, the Lord offered to provide him with a sign. But Ahaz feigned humility and refused, saying he would not test the Lord.

13. HOUSE OF DAVID: The prophet, upon hearing Ahaz's refusal, now broadens his audience beyond Ahaz to include the whole faithless house of David. The entire nation was guilty of wearying God.

14. THE LORD HIMSELF WILL GIVE YOU A SIGN: Ahaz refused to choose a sign, so the Lord now states that He will send His own sign. The implementation of this prophecy would not take place until long after Ahaz's lifetime.

THE VIRGIN: This prophecy reached forward to the virgin birth of the Messiah, as the New Testament writers note (see Matthew 1:23). The Hebrew word refers to an unmarried woman and means "virgin" (see Genesis 24:43; Proverbs 30:19; Song of Solomon 1:3; 6:8), so the birth of Isaiah's own son (see Isaiah 8:3) could not have fully satisfied the prophecy.

IMMANUEL: The title, applied to Jesus, means "God with us."

15. CURDS AND HONEY: Curds result from coagulated milk and resemble something like cottage cheese. This diet indicated the scarcity of provisions that characterized the period after the foreign invaders had decimated the land.

16. REFUSE THE EVIL: Before the promised son of Isaiah was old enough to make moral choices, the kings of Syria and Ephraim were to meet their doom at the hands of the Assyrians.

17. BRING THE KING OF ASSYRIA UPON YOU: Not only did the Lord use the Assyrians to judge the northern kingdom, He also used that nation to invade Ahaz's domain of Judah. This coming of the Assyrian king was the beginning of the end for the nation, and it eventually led to the captivity of her people in Babylon.

18–25. IT SHALL COME TO PASS: The desolation prophesied in this section began in the days of Ahaz and reached its climax when the Babylonians conquered Judah. Its results continue to the time when the Messiah will return to deliver Israel and establish His kingdom on earth.

FLY . . . BEE: Egypt was full of flies, and Assyria was a country noted for beekeeping. These insects represented the armies from the powerful countries that the Lord would summon to overrun Judah and take the people into exile.

19. DESOLATE VALLEYS . . . CLEFTS OF THE ROCKS: Not even the inaccessible areas of the land would be free from the invading armies.

20. HIRED RAZOR: The Assyrians were the Lord's hired blade to shave and disgrace the entire body of Judah.

21. YOUNG COW AND TWO SHEEP: The foreign invasion would cause a change from an agricultural economy to a pastoral one. Not enough people would remain in the land to farm. It was to be a time of great poverty.

23–25. BRIERS AND THORNS. The presence of these uncultivated plants was a sign of desolation.

Read Isaiah 9:1–11:16, noting the key words and phrases indicated below.

> A VISION OF LIGHT: *Isaiah's prophecies continue to extend beyond the immediate future of his listeners and point to the coming of Jesus as the Messiah.*

9:1. THE LAND OF ZEBULUN AND . . . NAPHTALI: Zebulun and Naphtali, located on the northern border in northeast Galilee west of the Jordan River, were the first to suffer from the invasion by the Assyrian king (see 2 Kings 15:29). This marked the beginning of dark days for Israel.

MORE HEAVILY OPPRESSED HER: A better translation is "will glorify her." "At first" the days were to be full of gloom, but "afterward" God would transform that gloom into honor. The New Testament authors apply this prophecy of Galilee's honor to the arrival of Jesus (see Matthew 4:12–16). Ultimately, the fulfillment of this prophecy will occur at Jesus' Second Advent, when the area is freed from the yoke of foreign invaders.

2. A GREAT LIGHT: The coming of the Messiah is synonymous with the coming of light to remove the darkness of captivity.

3. MULTIPLIED THE NATION: Once again, the Lord confirms His covenant with Abraham to multiply his physical descendants as the sands of the seashore (see Genesis 22:17).

4. BROKEN THE YOKE: Eventually, the Lord will free national Israel from bondage to Assyria, Babylon, and every other foreign power that has oppressed her.

5. BURNING AND FUEL OF FIRE: The world will no longer need the accessories of warfare because a time of universal peace will follow the return of Christ.

6. UNTO US A CHILD IS BORN . . . A SON: These terms elaborate further on Immanuel, the child to be born to the virgin. The virgin's child will also be the royal Son of David, with rights to the Davidic throne (see Matthew 1:21; Luke 1:31–33; 2:7, 11).

THE GOVERNMENT: The Son will rule the nations of the world (see Revelation 2:27; 19:15).

WONDERFUL, COUNSELOR: The remaining three titles each consist of two words, so the intention was likely that each pair of words indicate one title. Here, the title would be "Wonderful Counselor." In contrast to Ahaz, this King will implement supernatural wisdom in discharging His office.

MIGHTY GOD: As a powerful warrior, the Messiah will accomplish the military exploits mentioned in Isaiah 9:3–5.

EVERLASTING FATHER: The Messiah will be a Father to His people eternally. As Davidic King, He will compassionately care for and discipline them.

PRINCE OF PEACE: The government of Immanuel will procure and perpetuate peace among the nations of the world.

7. THRONE OF DAVID: The virgin's Son will be the rightful heir to David's throne and will inherit the promises of the Davidic covenant.

POETIC JUSTICE: The next section of Isaiah's prophecy includes a poem that describes future judgments against both Samaria and Assyria.

8. SENT A WORD AGAINST JACOB: This poem (through 10:4) tells of warning calamities sent by the Lord that have gone unheeded by Israel.

9. PRIDE AND ARROGANCE: Israel's downfall was her feeling of self-sufficiency, whereby she thought she could handle any eventuality.

11. ADVERSARIES OF REZIN: The Syrian king's enemies were the Assyrians.

12. HIS HAND IS STRETCHED OUT STILL: God's outstretched hand will punish beyond what the people had already experienced.

16. LEADERS . . . THOSE WHO ARE LED: The aggravated wickedness of Israel extended to all classes, even the fatherless and widows, who often were the objects of special mercy.

19. NO MAN . . . HIS BROTHER: God's wrath allowed wickedness to cause the society to self-destruct. A senseless, mutual exploitation resulted in anarchy and confusion.

21. MANASSEH . . . EPHRAIM . . . JUDAH: The descendants of Joseph's two sons, Manasseh and Ephraim, had engaged in civil war with one another before (see Judges 12:4). They would unite only in their opposition to Judah.

> ASSYRIA SHALL BE JUDGED: *The nation of Assyria would serve as God's instrument of judgment for His people's rebellion. But Assyria would also be judged for her sins.*

10:2. UNRIGHTEOUS DECREES . . . ROB THE NEEDY: The prophet returns to assigning reasons for God's wrath: (1) the people's inequities in administering the laws, and (2) their harsh treatment of those in need.

3. DAY OF PUNISHMENT: The Assyrians would be the first to invade, but Babylon and other foreign powers would follow.

5. ROD OF MY ANGER: God used Assyria as His instrument of judgment against Israel and Judah. He would later do the same with Babylon against Judah (see Habakkuk 1:6).

6. AN UNGODLY NATION: "My people" (verse 2) refers to the people of Israel and Judah.

7. HE DOES NOT MEAN SO: Assyria did not realize she was the Lord's instrument but thought her conquests were the result of her own power.

9. CALNO . . . DAMASCUS: Cities and territories that capitulated to the Assyrian invaders.

11. SHALL I NOT DO ALSO: Proud Assyria warned Jerusalem that she would overcome that city just as she had been the instrument used by God against other nations.

12. PUNISH . . . THE KING OF ASSYRIA: God expresses His intention of punishing proud Assyria after He has finished using that nation to punish Jerusalem.

13–14. I HAVE DONE IT: The prophet proved the Assyrian king's pride by reiterating his boast.

15. AX . . . SAW . . . ROD . . . STAFF: Assyria was nothing more than an instrument of the Lord and had no power or wisdom of her own.

16–19. CONSUME THE GLORY: When God had finished using Assyria as His instrument, He would terminate the kingdom's existence.

> FUTURE HOPE: *God proclaims that a remnant of His people will be saved and that the future Messiah will bring ultimate salvation to the world.*

20. REMNANT OF ISRAEL: A small nucleus of God's people, preserved by His sovereign grace, would form a righteous remnant in the midst of the national apostasy. In Israel's history, there were always an obedient few who preserved, obeyed, and passed on God's Law. There will always be a remnant, because God will never forsake the Abrahamic covenant.

23. A DETERMINED END: The people must face the wrath of God. The apostle Paul would later draw on this verse when he wrote, "He will finish the work and cut it short in righteousness, because the LORD will make a short work upon the earth" (Romans 9:28).

25. THE INDIGNATION WILL CEASE: The indignation covers the entire period of Israel's exile (see Daniel 11:36). Here is the promise that it will end with the return of the Messiah.

26. MIDIAN . . . EGYPT: Isaiah selects two examples from the past to illustrate the Lord's future deliverance of Israel: (1) Gideon's victory over the Midianites (see Judges 7:25), and (2) the slaughter of the Egyptians who pursued the Israelites through the Red Sea (see Exodus 14:16, 26–27).

27. THE YOKE WILL BE DESTROYED: The removal of this yoke speaks of the future freeing of Israel from compulsion to render service to foreign oppressors.

28. HE HAS COME: Isaiah visualizes the Assyrian army approaching Jerusalem from the north. The place names grow closer to Jerusalem as his vision progresses.

33. LOP OFF THE BOUGH: Although the Assyrian army would reach the walls of Jerusalem, the sovereign Lord would intervene and send them away

in defeat. Later, Isaiah recorded the literal fulfillment of this prophecy (see Isaiah 37:24, 36–38).

34. LEBANON: The Old Testament equates Assyria with Lebanon (see, for example, Ezekiel 31:3).

> JESSE'S OFFSPRING: *Isaiah returns to his discussion of the coming Messiah, who would spring forth from the "root" of Jesse, the father of King David.*

11:1. STEM . . . ROOTS: With the Babylonian captivity of 586 BC, the Davidic dynasty appeared as decimated as the Assyrian army. The major difference between the two was the life remaining in the stump and roots of the Davidic line. This life was to manifest itself in new growth in the form of the Rod and Branch.

JESSE: David's father, through whose line the messianic king was to come.

BRANCH: A title for the Messiah (see Isaiah 4:2).

2. THE SPIRIT OF THE LORD: As the Spirit of the Lord came upon David when he was anointed king (see 1 Samuel 16:13), so He will rest upon David's descendant, Christ, who will rule the world. The Messiah's Spirit-imparted qualities will enable Him to rule justly and effectively.

3. SIGHT OF HIS EYES . . . HEARING OF HIS EARS: These are the usual avenues for a king to obtain the information needed to govern, but the future King will have supernatural perception that goes beyond these typical sources.

4. DECIDE WITH EQUITY: The Messiah will reverse Israel's earlier dealings with the underprivileged (see Isaiah 3:14, 15; 10:2).

ROD OF HIS MOUTH. The Branch's rule over the nations will be forceful. The New Testament authors use equivalent terminology to describe the Warrior-King at His triumphant return to earth (see, for example, Revelation 19:15).

BREATH OF HIS LIPS: This is another figure of speech that refers to the Messiah's means of inflicting physical harm. Paul would later draw on this verse to reveal the destruction of the man of lawlessness at Christ's Second Advent (see 2 Thessalonians 2:8).

5. THE BELT: The belt, which gathered the loose garments together, is figurative of the Messiah's readiness for conflict. Righteousness and faithfulness are His preparation.

6. THE WOLF . . . THE LAMB: Conditions of peace will prevail to the extent that all enmity among humans, among animals, and between humans and animals, will disappear. Such will characterize the future millennial kingdom in which the Prince of Peace will reign.

9. FULL OF THE KNOWLEDGE OF THE LORD: Everyone will know the Lord when He returns to fulfill His New Covenant with Israel (see Jeremiah 31:34).

10. IN THAT DAY: The time of universal peace will come in the future reign of the Lord.

GENTILES SHALL SEEK HIM: The Root of Jesse will also attract non-Jews who inhabit the future kingdom. Paul saw God's ministry to Gentiles during the church age as an additional implication of this verse (see Romans 15:12).

11. SECOND TIME: The first return of Israel to her land was from Egyptian captivity (see Exodus 14:26–29). The second will be from her worldwide dispersion (see Isaiah 51:9–11).

12. FOUR CORNERS OF THE EARTH. This figurative expression depicts the whole world. The faithful remnant of Israel will return from a worldwide dispersion to their land.

13. EPHRAIM . . . JUDAH: The two major divisions of Israel after the schism under Jeroboam (see 1 Kings 12:16–20). Ephraim was the name representing the ten northern tribes, and Judah the two southern tribes. When the Messiah returns, they will reunite in a lasting peace.

14. WEST . . . EAST: In that day, Israel will be free from all foreign oppression and will be the dominant political force.

15. THE RIVER: Just as God dried up the Red Sea in His deliverance of the Israelites from Egypt, so He will dry up the Euphrates River in connection with the final deliverance of His people.

16. HIGHWAY: Isaiah has much to say about a way for the remnant returning to Jerusalem (see Isaiah 35:8–9; 42:16; 43:19; 48:21; 49:11; 57:14; 62:10).

UNLEASHING THE TEXT

1) What is the predominant theme of Isaiah's prophecies in these chapters?

_____

_____

_____

_____

2) Looking at Isaiah 7, what can you learn from about the life and ministry of the Messiah?

_____

_____

_____

_____

_____

3) Which elements of Isaiah 9:1–7 has Jesus already fulfilled? Which promises are still to come?

_____

_____

_____

_____

_____

4) Why is it significant that the Messiah would come "from the stem of Jesse," the father of King David (see Matthew 1:1–17)?

_____

_____

_____

_____

_____

_____

EXPLORING THE MEANING

We can always take God at His word. Isaiah 7 includes a somewhat humorous moment that is often overlooked. God wanted to reassure the people of Jerusalem that they did need not to fear the threat of Syria, Ephraim (another name for the northern kingdom of Israel), or Assyria. So He encouraged Ahaz, the king of Judah, to ask for a sign as proof that deliverance would come. God wanted to encourage Ahaz's faith as well as that of the people in Jerusalem.

However, Ahaz feigned humility in refusing the sign: "But Ahaz said, 'I will not ask, nor will I test the LORD!'" (verse 12). The king refused to do what God asked. Ironically, in professing his desire to avoid testing God, he drifted into direct disobedience of God!

False piety might win us the praise of men, but God is never fooled by it— He knows even better than we do what is really going on in our hearts and what is motivating our actions. As we come to learn, God responded to Ahaz's refusal to ask for a sign of temporary salvation by giving a sign of His permanent salvation to come. Through Isaiah, God declared, "Behold, the virgin shall conceive and bear a Son, and shall call His name Immanuel" (verse 14). This specific sign referred to the future birth of Jesus, which was and is a blessing for all people.

Biblical prophecy typically involves layers. The Old Testament contains many passages that point forward to the life and ministry of Jesus. But few are better known than Isaiah 9:6–7:

> For unto us a Child is born,
> Unto us a Son is given;
> And the government will be upon His shoulder.
> And His name will be called
> Wonderful, Counselor, Mighty God,
> Everlasting Father, Prince of Peace.
> Of the increase of His government and peace
> There will be no end,
> Upon the throne of David and over His kingdom,
> To order it and establish it with judgment and justice
> From that time forward, even forever.
> The zeal of the LORD of hosts will perform this.

Reading these verses, it's clear that many aspects of this Messianic prophecy have already been fulfilled by Christ. The phrase "unto us a Child is born," for example, points back to Jesus' miraculous birth, which Isaiah had already promised in chapter 7. In addition, Jesus was demonstrably a descendent of David (see Matthew 1:1–17), and throughout the New Testament the authors affirmed Him to be "Mighty God."

However, several aspects of Isaiah's prophecy are yet to be fulfilled. For instance, we know from Scripture that Jesus will one day take the government upon His shoulders (see Revelation 2:27; 19:15). However, we are also painfully aware that this has not yet taken place. Similarly, Jesus has not yet brought "peace" to the world, nor has He established His perfect "justice." Those promises will be fulfilled at the end of history.

These verses shine a light on the complexity of biblical prophecy and the need for careful, objective interpretation. The people of Jesus' day were fixated on the temporal fulfillment of Isaiah's prophecies and longed for a leader to free them from Rome's oppressive rulers. Therefore, they sought only a Messiah who would take the reins of David's throne as a military King. Their skewed view of Isaiah's prophecies ultimately led them to reject Christ as their true Messiah and cry out for His execution (see Matthew 27:22). Your priorities and timetables likewise won't always match up with God's, and you shouldn't expect all His promises and blessings to arrive according to your schedule.

We can be confident of a glorious future. The Old Testament prophets were often viewed as "speakers of doom" who constantly railed about bad news and coming judgment. Yet much of Isaiah's prophetic words were incredibly hopeful and inspiring—especially when he spoke of the future that God has prepared for His people.

In speaking of "that day" when the Messiah will fully reveal His authority in the universe, Isaiah proclaimed, "The wolf also shall dwell with the lamb, the leopard shall lie down with the young goat, the calf and the young lion and the fatling together; and a little child shall lead them. . . . They shall not hurt nor destroy in all My holy mountain, for the earth shall be full of the knowledge of the LORD as the waters cover the sea" (11:6–9).

Isaiah was describing a future time of universal peace under the leadership of Jesus in His millennial kingdom. His words point forward to the same blessed hope the apostle John describes in Revelation 21: "And I heard a loud voice from heaven saying, 'Behold, the tabernacle of God is with men, and He will dwell with them, and they shall be His people. God Himself will be with them and be their God. And God will wipe away every tear from their eyes; there shall be no more death, nor sorrow, nor crying. There shall be no more pain, for the former things have passed away" (verses 3–4).

REFLECTING ON THE TEXT

5) How should Ahaz have responded when God offered to give him a sign? Why was his response both disobedient and hypocritical?

_____

_____

_____

_____

_____

_____

6) What helps you to have confidence that God will fulfill His promises in the Bible?

_____

_____

_____

_____

_____

7) What is the danger of looking for God to fulfill His promises according to your own priorities?

_____

_____

_____

_____

_____

8) How do God's promises for the future bring you comfort today?

_____

_____

_____

_____

_____

PERSONAL RESPONSE

9) What is the danger of false piety? How do you combat the hypocritical desire to be seen as "pious" or "spiritual" by others??

_____

_____

_____

_____

_____

_____

_____

10) What steps can you take this week to reject the allure of this world and its temporary pleasure and fix your heart on the future God has prepared for you?

_____

_____

_____

_____

_____

_____

_____

3

JUDGMENT AGAINST BABYLON AND ASSYRIA

Isaiah 13:1–15:19; 17:1–14

DRAWING NEAR

How would you summarize your thoughts and attitudes toward those who are hostile to you and your faith?

_____

_____

_____

_____

_____

_____

_____

_____

THE CONTEXT

Isaiah was called by God around 739 BC, and his prophetic ministry extended for nearly sixty years. As we have seen, that period was marked by danger and upheaval among the nations around Judah and its capital city of Jerusalem. In the previous lesson, we explored the immediate danger to Judah posed by the military alliance between Israel and Syria, which God declared would come to nothing.

In this lesson, Isaiah's prophecies address two key nations that would come to play a major role in the history of God's people: Babylon and Assyria. During the time of Isaiah's ministry, Assyria was already a major player on the world stage. It was a warrior nation known for its brutality and bloodthirsty desire for conquest. It would not be long before it conquered the northern kingdom of Israel (in 722 BC) and led her people into captivity. Babylon had not yet become a major power, but it was a known enemy on the world scene.

More than a century after Isaiah's ministry, in 597 BC, Nebuchadnezzar II of Babylon led a military campaign against Judah. He laid siege to Jerusalem and ultimately conquered it. He then destroyed Jerusalem—a terrible moment in the history of God's people. Yet in the chapters under study here, Isaiah prophetically spoke of Babylon's ultimate judgment and destruction at God's hands. Additionally, Isaiah's prophecies revealed how Assyria would serve as a rod of punishment for the Lord's plans, destroying nations such as Philistia, Moab, Syria, and—as noted above—even the northern kingdom of Israel.

KEYS TO THE TEXT

Read Isaiah 13:1–15:9, noting the key words and phrases indicated below.

> *JUDGMENT AGAINST BABYLON: Isaiah now begins to relate God's judgments against the nations. Although Babylon was not yet a major power at the time, Isaiah foresaw a time when it would overthrow Assyria and be an international force.*

13:1. THE BURDEN: Used in the sense of Isaiah's having a heavy responsibility to deliver the message. It is used fifteen other times in the Old Testament in superscriptions like this.

AGAINST BABYLON: Isaiah's prophecy in this chapter foretells the city's destruction. Even during the time of the Assyrian Empire, the dominant power of the time, the city of Babylon was formidable and stood at the head of the list of Israel's enemies to be conquered.

2–3. LIFT UP A BANNER: The Lord summons foreign armies to conquer Babylon in all her greatness.

3. MY ANGER: God's anger had turned away from Israel (see Isaiah 12:1) and toward this oppressive foreign power.

4. THE LORD OF HOSTS MUSTERS THE ARMY: Literally, "the LORD of armies musters the army." This prophecy looks to the end-time coming of the

Lord to crush the final Babylon, dash His enemies in pieces, and establish a kingdom over all nations (se Revelation 19:11–16).

5. FROM THE END OF HEAVEN: The fall of Babylon to the Medes was merely a short-term glimpse of the ultimate fall of Babylon at the hands of the universal forces of God (see Revelation 18:2).

6. THE DAY OF THE LORD IS AT HAND: This prophecy looks beyond the immediate conquest of the city by the Medes to a greater day of the Lord. It anticipates the final destruction of Babylon by the intervention of the Messiah.

7. HEART WILL MELT: Courage was to vanish.

8. IN PAIN AS A WOMAN IN CHILDBIRTH: This comparison of labor pains is often a figure to describe human sufferings in the period just before the final deliverance of Israel. Usually, this depicts the suffering of Israel, but here Isaiah pictures the misery of Babylon.

9. DAY OF THE LORD: As in verse 6, this occurs when the Messiah returns in judgment over all living on earth. In this case, the prophet moves forward to the "final Babylon," which is the final evil world city to be destroyed with all its inhabitants (see Revelation 17–18).

10. STARS . . . SUN . . . MOON: Scripture frequently associates cosmic upheavals with the period of tribulation just before Christ's return (see, for example, Ezekiel 32:7–8; Joel 2:10, 30–31; Matthew 24:29; Mark 13:24–25; Luke 21:25; Revelation 6:12–14).

11 I WILL HALT THE ARROGANCE: The same sin of pride that led to Israel's judgment will cause Babylon's downfall.

12. A MORTAL MORE RARE THAN FINE GOLD: Because of this visitation, human mortality will be extremely high, but not total. God will spare a faithful remnant.

13. SHAKE THE HEAVENS: These upheavals are associated with the ones in verse 10.

14. GAZELLE . . . SHEEP: Humans are frightening to the shy gazelle, but indispensable to the helpless sheep. The Babylonians will find the Lord as their enemy and lose Him as their shepherd. All they can do is flee the land.

15–16. THRUST THROUGH: The prophet returns to the immediate future, when the Medes will commit all those cruel atrocities in captured Babylon.

17. MEDES: This people group was from an area southwest of the Caspian Sea, north of Persia, east of Assyria, and northeast of Babylon. They later allied

themselves with the Babylonians to conquer Assyria (c. 610 BC) and with the Persians to conquer Babylon (539 BC).

19–22. AND BABYLON: In Isaiah now moves from events in the near future to the distant future. The ultimate fulfillment of these prophecies of Babylon's desolation will come in conjunction with Babylon's rebuilding and utter destruction when Christ returns (see Revelation 14:8; 18:2). Obviously, Isaiah was unable to see the many centuries that separated Babylon's fall to the Medes from the destruction of the final Babylon by God (see Revelation 17–18).

19. SODOM AND GOMORRAH: God will overthrow rebuilt Babylon in the same supernatural way that He did these two ancient cities (see Genesis 19:24; Revelation 18:8).

20. NEVER BE INHABITED: Though nothing like its glorious past, the site of Babylon has never been void of inhabitants. A city or town of one type or another has always existed there, so this prophecy must point toward a yet future desolation.

21–22. WILD BEASTS: This utter devastation is further described in Revelation 18:2.

22. NEAR TO COME: Once Babylon becomes great, her days are numbered.

FALL OF BABYLON: *Isaiah again looks forward to the fall of the "final Babylon" at the end of the tribulation. This will result in the deliverance of Israel from bondage.*

14:1. MERCY ON JACOB: Although this passage has some reference to the people of Judah's release from Babylonian captivity, the primary view in mind is identified in these opening verses (through verse 3). Isaiah looks to the final Babylon at the end of the tribulation. The language is that which characterizes conditions during the millennial kingdom after the judgment of the final Babylon. The destruction of future Babylon is integrally connected with the deliverance of Israel from bondage. Babylon must perish so that the Lord may exalt His people.

THE STRANGERS: These are Jewish proselytes who join themselves to the nation in the final earthly kingdom of Christ.

2. TAKE THEM CAPTIVE WHOSE CAPTIVES THEY WERE: Here is the great role reversal. Instead of the Israelites' miserable state of captivity, endured during

the tribulation under Antichrist, they will be the rulers of those nations that once dominated them.

3. REST: The future earthly kingdom of the Messiah is in view (see Acts 3:19–21).

4. YOU WILL TAKE UP THIS PROVERB: The prophet instructs the people of the delivered nation to sing the song of verses 4–21, celebrating the downfall of the king of Babylon.

THE KING OF BABYLON. This could refer to the final Antichrist, who will rule Babylon, which will rule the earth (see Revelation 17:17, 18).

OPPRESSOR HAS CEASED: The nation that made life bitter for God's people has disappeared.

6. STRUCK THE PEOPLE: This pictures the tyranny of the Babylonian king.

7. THE WHOLE EARTH . . . AT REST AND QUIET: With the tyrant off the throne, the whole world will have peace. This again represents millennial conditions.

10. HAVE YOU BECOME LIKE US?: The kings mock the king of Babylon, reminding him that human distinctions are meaningless among the dead.

11. YOUR POMP IS BROUGHT DOWN TO SHEOL: Those kings of the nations already in the place of the dead stage a welcome party for the arriving king of Babylon.

THE MAGGOT: Human pride vanishes for a rotting corpse covered with worms.

THE FALL OF LUCIFER: Isaiah continues to speak against the king of Babylon, but now shifts to address the one who was empowering him behind the scenes.

12. HOW YOU ARE FALLEN: Jesus' use of this verse to describe Satan's fall (see Luke 10:18) has led many to see more than a reference in Isaiah's words to the king of Babylon. Just as the Lord addressed Satan in His words to the serpent (see Genesis 3:14–15), this inspired dirge speaks to the king of Babylon and to the devil who was energizing him. (See Ezekiel 28:12–17 for similar language to the king of Tyre and Satan behind him.)

HEAVEN: The scene suddenly shifts from the underworld to heaven to emphasize the unbridled pride of the king and of Satan, who was energizing him.

LUCIFER, SON OF THE MORNING: Lucifer literally means "shining one," but translators have often rendered it "morning star." The tradition of that time saw the stars as representing gods battling among themselves for places of preeminence.

13. I WILL: Five "I wills" in verses 13–14 emphasize the arrogance of the king of Babylon and of Satan, from whom he takes his cue.

MOUNT OF THE CONGREGATION: A mountain in northern Syria where, according to local tradition, the Canaanite gods assembled. The human king aspired to kingship over those gods.

15. SHEOL . . . THE PIT: Death awaits those who try to be like God (see Genesis 3:5, 22).

16–21. IS THIS THE MAN: The final section of Isaiah's dirge in this chapter elaborates on the disgrace of the king, on display before all as an unburied corpse. His complete role reversal, from preeminent power to utter humiliation, will provoke universal amazement.

18. ALL THE KINGS . . . SLEEP IN GLORY: The king of Babylon is the sole exception. The rest of the kings received honorable burials.

19. CORPSE TRODDEN UNDERFOOT: Among the ancients, this was the deepest degradation.

20. NEVER BE NAMED: Because the king of Babylon was an evildoer, he had no monument or posterity to keep his memory alive.

22. CUT OFF: Israel will have a remnant who are saved, but Babylon won't.

26. PURPOSE THAT IS PURPOSED: The scope of this judgment against the whole earth represents His final wrath against the ungodly in Israel and the nations.

JUDGMENT AGAINST PHILISTIA AND MOAB: Both of these nations were ancient enemies of God's people, and both would soon by overrun by Assyria. Their demise taught Israel not to depend on other nations but only on the Lord.

28. AHAZ DIED: The year of King Ahaz's death is uncertain. It came when Hezekiah began his reign, either in 727 BC (see 2 Kings 18:1, 9–10) or 716 BC (see 2 Kings 18:13).

29. PHILISTIA: Israel need not think that an alliance with the Philistines would save them from the Assyrians, since Assyria would conquer this neighbor of Israel as well.

ROD . . . BROKEN: The prophet pictures the Assyrian weakness, their conquest of Philistia notwithstanding.

30. POOR: The poor of Judah who depend on the Lord will find Him to be a refuge, but the Philistine oppressors are to meet their doom.

32. MESSENGERS OF THE NATION: These were Philistine envoys who sought an alliance with Israel. Isaiah's answer saw the Lord as Zion's only security.

15:1. MOAB: Moab was a country about thirty miles square, east of the Dead Sea, south of the Arnon River, and north of the Zered River.

AR . . . KIR: The two major cities of Moab.

2. UP TO THE TEMPLE AND DIBON: The Moabites chose the temple of the Moabite god Chemosh—located three miles north of the Arnon River—as the place of weeping because that god had failed to deliver the nation.

NEBO . . . MEDEBA: Nebo is the mountain at the north end of the Dead Sea, east of the Jordan River, where the Lord took Moses to view the Promised Land (see Deuteronomy 34:1). Medeba is five miles southeast of Nebo.

BALDNESS . . . EVERY BEARD: Shaving heads and beards expressed disgrace and humiliation (see Leviticus 21:5; Jeremiah 41:5; 48:37).

3. CLOTHE THEMSELVES WITH SACKCLOTH: Wearing of sackcloth occurs forty-six times in the Bible as a sign of mourning.

4. HESHBON . . . ELEALEH . . . JAHAZ: The city of Heshbon was just under twenty miles east of the northern end of the Dead Sea in a territory claimed by both Israel and Moab (see Deuteronomy 2:32–33). Elealeh was about one mile away from Heshbon. Jahaz was more than ten miles south of Heshbon.

5. MY HEART WILL CRY OUT: This prophecy expresses much greater sympathy for Moab's plight than the other nations to be judged, even allowing for a surviving remnant (see Isaiah 16:11, 14).

A THREE-YEAR-OLD HEIFER: This phrase is actually the proper name of Eglath-shelishiyah, a city of unknown location.

LUHITH . . . HORONAIM: Two more cities whose locations are unknown.

6. NIMRIM: This is possibly the Wadi Numeira, the drying up of whose waters, along with the dead grass, pictures widespread devastation in Moab.

7. BROOK OF THE WILLOWS: This probably refers to the Zered River. The refugees from Moab had to cross this river into Edom to escape their invaders.

8. EGLAIM . . . BEER ELIM: The shouts of the fugitives will reach all the way from the northern part of Edom (Eglaim) to its southern extremity (Beer Elim).

9. DIMON: Perhaps another spelling of Dibon (see verse 2). This religious center of paganism is appropriate as a closing representation of the whole land of Moab.

LIONS UPON HIM WHO ESCAPES: Flight from invading armies would not bring security, but new dangers from the beasts of the wilderness.

Read Isaiah 17:1–14, noting the key words and phrases indicated below.

> JUDGMENT AGAINST SYRIA AND ISRAEL: *Assyria would conquer not only foreign nations, but even the northern kingdom of Israel (also called Ephraim).*

1. DAMASCUS: This city, sometimes called Aram, served as the capital of Syria. Its location northeast of Mount Hermon on the main land route between Mesopotamia and Egypt made it very influential. Its destruction by the Assyrians in 732 BC is the subject of this chapter.

2. AROER: Syria's domain extended as far south as Aroer, east of the Dead Sea, on the Arnon River (see 2 Kings 10:32–33).

3. FROM EPHRAIM: The northern ten tribes, also known as Israel, joined with Syria as objects of this oracle. They formed an alliance with Syria to combat the Assyrians, but many of their cites fell victim to the campaign in which Syria fell.

REMNANT OF SYRIA: Syria was to have a remnant (but not a kingdom) after the Assyrian onslaught.

4. GLORY OF JACOB: The waning of this glory pictures the judgment of God against the ten northern tribes, the descendants of Jacob.

5. VALLEY OF REPHAIM: As harvesters stripped bare that fertile valley west of Jerusalem, so God's judgment would leave nothing fruitful in the northern kingdom.

6. TWO OR THREE . . . FOUR OR FIVE: God's judgment against Ephraim was to leave only sparse pieces of her original abundance of olives.

7. LOOK TO HIS MAKER: In the future, severe judgments are to awaken a remnant of Ephraim to their failure to depend on the Lord. Then they will repent.

8. WORK OF HIS HANDS: Repentance is to lead to the forsaking of idolatry, which had for so long beset the nation.

10. FORGOTTEN . . . GOD: Failure to remember God had left Israel unprotected.

11. MAKE YOUR PLANT TO GROW: The prophet reminded his readers of the futility of trying to meet their needs without the Lord's help.

12. MULTITUDE OF MANY PEOPLE: The prophet now turns his attention to the coming armies of Judah's enemies and pronounces a "woe" upon them.

13. GOD WILL REBUKE THEM: God's rebuke will put those enemies to flight.

14. HE IS NO MORE: When morning comes, the invading force will have disappeared. God protects His people.

UNLEASHING THE TEXT

1) What images strike you in Isaiah's prophecy of Babylon's destruction?

_____

_____

_____

_____

_____

_____

2) Do you think the destruction of these nations should be a cause for sorrow or rejoicing? Explain.

_____

_____

_____

_____

3) Why would these prophecies of judgment against different nations have been important and even encouraging for the people of Isaiah's day?

_____

_____

_____

_____

4) What made Ephraim's betrayal particularly grievous? Why should they have known better?

_____

_____

_____

_____

_____

EXPLORING THE MEANING

God is Judge over all nations. The world of Isaiah's day was shaken by war and upheavals of many kinds, much like the world has been shaken by wars and tragedies for most of human history—including today. Many people view the reality of war and suffering as evidence against God's existence or essential goodness. They ask, "If God is real, why doesn't He put a stop to such terrible events?" In reality, war and suffering are not evidence of neglect or powerlessness on God's part. Rather, they are evidence of human sinfulness.

Even so, it is comforting to know that God does not hold Himself apart from or above the ravages of war, but actively maintains His authority as Judge over all nations. As He declared through Isaiah's prophecy, "I will punish the world for its evil, and the wicked for their iniquity; I will halt the arrogance of the proud, and will lay low the haughtiness of the terrible. I will make a mortal more rare than fine gold, a man more than the golden wedge of Ophir" (13:11–12).

We know from Scripture that God used Babylon as a tool to punish the people of Judah for their rebellion against Him. As God said through the prophet Jeremiah, "Behold, I will make you a terror to yourself and to all your friends; and they shall fall by the sword of their enemies, and your eyes shall see it. I will give all Judah into the hand of the king of Babylon, and he shall carry them captive to Babylon and slay them with the sword" (Jeremiah 20:4). Yet Isaiah's prophecy makes it clear that, on God's authority, Babylon would itself be judged and destroyed because of its own wickedness.

God is Judge over all evil. Not only does God exercise His authority to judge evil nations and kings, but He also judges evil in every instance and from every source—including Satan himself. In Isaiah 14, the prophet was describing the future fall of the king of Babylon when he suddenly made this statement: "How you are fallen from heaven, O Lucifer, son of the morning! How you are cut down to the ground, you who weakened the nations! For you have said in your heart: 'I will ascend into heaven, I will exalt my throne above the stars of God . . . I will be like the Most High'" (verses 12–14).

Many see in Isaiah's words a twofold denunciation. The prophet was still speaking of the humiliation and defeat awaiting Babylon's king. Yet he also was making a distinct connection between that king and Satan—the evil power behind the scenes. He is the "prince of the power of the air" (Ephesians 2:2) and "the great dragon . . . who deceives the whole world" (Revelation 12:9). Isaiah showed that Babylon's evil was directly connected to Satan and was a reflection of his ongoing rebellion against God.

Of course, the wonderful news is that Satan is a *defeated* foe. Neither he nor evil will win the day in the end because Jesus has already won the victory through His death and resurrection on the cross. As John declared, "I heard a loud voice saying in heaven, 'Now salvation, and strength, and the kingdom of our God, and the power of His Christ have come, for the accuser of our brethren, who accused them before our God day and night, has been cast down. And they overcame him by the blood of the Lamb and by the word of their testimony, and they did not love their lives to the death'" (Revelation 12:10–11).

God will judge all people. For the original hearers of Isaiah's prophecy, much of what the prophet related in chapters 13–16 was good news. The people of Judah likely applauded word of a coming judgment against Babylon and Assyria. Similarly, they would have been glad to hear about the destruction of Philistia and Syria. Even the Moabites were ancient enemies.

However, this attitude would have changed when the prophet declared, "'The fortress also will cease from Ephraim, the kingdom from Damascus, and the remnant of Syria; they will be as the glory of the children of Israel,' says the LORD of hosts. 'In that day it shall come to pass that the glory of Jacob will wane, and the fatness of his flesh grow lean'" (17:3–4).

During Isaiah's day, the nations of Israel and Judah were in conflict. Yet they were still united by a common heritage—a common identity as God's chosen people. Therefore, it would have likely come as a great shock for the people of Judah to hear God pronouncing judgment against their brothers and sisters in Israel. Many of the Jewish people in the Old Testament believed that their status as "chosen" would protect them against God's wrath, in spite of their idolatry and rebellion against Him. Of course, they were wrong.

Similarly, many people today believe they are immune from God's judgment because they identify themselves as "Christians," or because they believe they have done more good than bad things in their lives. In reality, Scripture makes it clear that God will judge all people, with no exceptions (see 1 Peter 4:5). Only those who have been washed in the blood of Christ through His free gift of salvation will be declared exempt from God's wrath.

REFLECTING ON THE TEXT

5) Where do you see evidence today that God remains sovereign over all nations and all people?

_____

_____

_____

_____

_____

_____

6) How would you describe Satan to someone unfamiliar with the Bible? Who is he? What does he want?

_____

_____

_____

_____

7) How does Satan wield influence through the evil of this world? What can God's people do to stand against it?

_____

_____

_____

_____

_____

8) Why is it critical to understand the truth that God will judge every person without exception?

_____

_____

_____

_____

_____

_____

_____

PERSONAL RESPONSE

9) What are some specific steps you can take today to limit the influence of Satan
and evil in your life?

_____

_____

_____

_____

_____

_____

_____

10) What are some ways that you can be an example to those who oppose you and
your faith?

_____

_____

_____

_____

_____

_____

_____

4

JUDGMENT AGAINST OTHER NATIONS
Isaiah 18:1–22:25

DRAWING NEAR
What comes to mind when you hear the word *judgment*? Explain.

_____

_____

_____

_____

_____

_____

_____

THE CONTEXT
In the previous lesson, we noted how Isaiah's prophecies included several predictions about nations beyond the borders of the kingdoms of Israel and Judah. Isaiah focused first on future judgments against Babylon and Assyria, two nations that would play a major role in the history of God's people by conquering Judah and Israel, respectively. Isaiah also related judgments from God on the smaller nations of Moab, Syria, and even the kingdom of Israel.

In this lesson, we will watch as Isaiah's prophetic gaze continues to swing across the world known by his original hearers. We will discover yet another round of prophetic judgments spoken against Babylon, but also against other powerful nations of the day, including Ethiopia (Cush), Egypt, Arabia, and Tyre. These pronouncements would likely have been received as good news by

Isaiah's original hearers in Judah. However, Isaiah 22 also includes a proclamation of judgment against *Jerusalem*, the heart of the promised land.

KEYS TO THE TEXT

Read Isaiah 18:1–22:25, noting the key words and phrases indicated below.

> *JUDGMENT AGAINST ETHIOPIA AND EGYPT: Isaiah's prophecies*
> *extend beyond Judah and its immediate neighbors to the nations*
> *of Ethiopia (Cush) and Egypt.*

18:1 BUZZING WINGS: These may speak of Ethiopia's strong armada of ships.

ETHIOPIA: "Cush" renders literally the Hebrew word for Ethiopia. The country was south of Egypt, including territory belonging to modern Ethiopia.

2. SEA . . . WATERS . . . RIVERS: These apparently refer to the Nile River and its tributaries.

3. ALL INHABITANTS . . . AND DWELLERS: The prophet calls on the entire human race to be alert for the signals that God is at work in the world.

4. I WILL TAKE MY REST: The Lord will wait patiently, until the appropriate time, to intervene in human affairs, until sunshine and dew have built to an opportune, climactic moment.

5. CUT OFF: As an all-wise farmer, God's pruning activity (His direct intervention) will be neither too early nor too late.

6. BIRDS OF PREY: Dropping his metaphorical language, Isaiah describes in grotesque language the fallen carcasses of the victims of God's judgment.

7. PLACE OF THE NAME OF THE LORD: Jerusalem remains the location on earth where the Lord has chosen to dwell. Isaiah's prophecy extends to the future bringing of tribute to Jerusalem in the Messiah's kingdom.

19:1. BURDEN AGAINST EGYPT: Isaiah now describes God's judgments against Egypt.

RIDES ON A SWIFT CLOUD: Clouds are figurative vehicles for the Lord's coming to execute judgment (see Psalms 18:10–11; 104:3; Daniel 7:13).

2. EGYPTIANS AGAINST EGYPTIANS: The nation, which was already noted for its internal strife through the centuries, will experience even worse under God's judgment.

3. MEDIUMS . . . SORCERERS: With nowhere else to turn, the Egyptians will consult spiritualists. Scripture reveals that the Israelites of Isaiah's day did the same (see Isaiah 8:19).

4. FIERCE KING: Egypt was subject to foreign rule, beginning with the Assyrian conquest of the middle-seventh century BC.

5. WASTED AND DRIED UP: God will take away the country's only water resource, the Nile and its tributaries.

7. SOWN BY THE RIVER: The alluvial deposits left by the flooding of the Nile yielded rich agricultural crops, permitting Egypt to export grain to the rest of the world.

8. CAST HOOKS . . . SPREAD NETS: The loss of the Nile's important fishing business would mean a great loss to Egypt's population.

9. FINE FLAX . . . FINE FABRIC: Egypt was famous for its production of linen from flax. Both the growth of the plant and the manufacture of the cloth depended on water.

10. FOUNDATIONS: God was to remove the "pillars" on which the working class depended. The word generally refers either to the economic structure of the society or specifically to the upper class, which organized the businesses of the land.

11–15. THE PRINCES: God's judgment was to confound Egypt's famed wisdom.

11. ZOAN: This major city of northern Egypt, east of the Nile Delta region, was the first large city a Semite would encounter in traveling toward the Nile. Tanis was also a name of this city. It was a capital of northern Egypt at one point when the country split into two parts.

12. WHERE ARE YOUR WISE MEN?: Egypt's experts were helpless to deal with the current crisis because they were ignorant of the Lord's judgment against the land.

13. NOPH: This is another name for Memphis, the capital of northern Egypt at one time. This city had leaders who were in a state of confusion about a true perspective on Egypt's crisis.

MAINSTAY OF ITS TRIBES: If the cornerstones of a society suffer from delusion, they can do nothing else than delude the people they lead.

14. THE LORD HAS MINGLED: The Lord would cause dizziness that resulted in a complete loss of productivity when the invaders came.

A FUTURE BLESSING: Isaiah now describes Egypt's eventual turning to the true God "in that day," referring to the time of the millennial rule of Christ. These features have not been true of Egypt yet.

16. WOMEN . . . BE AFRAID AND FEAR: God's judgment will immobilize mighty Egypt to the point that the nation realizes it is defenseless and helpless.

17. JUDAH WILL BE A TERROR TO EGYPT: Instead Judah fearing Egypt, the reverse will be true. God's great power on behalf of Israel will cause this to happen. Such will occur at Christ's Second Advent when He returns to this world.

18. FIVE CITIES: Humanly speaking, the chances of even one Egyptian city turning to the Lord were remote, but divinely speaking, there will be five times that many.

LANGUAGE OF CANAAN: Egypt is to speak the language of Judah. Not only are they to fear Judah, but they are also to convert to Judah's form of worship.

SWEAR BY THE LORD OF HOSTS: Egypt will, "in that day," turn to God in a dramatic way. This prophecy anticipates the personal reign of the Davidic King on earth.

CITY OF DESTRUCTION: This was likely the "City of the Sun" (Heliopolis), which was the home of the Egyptian sun god.

19. AN ALTAR . . . AND A PILLAR TO THE LORD: These speak figuratively of Egypt's conversion to the Lord "in that day" of the Messiah's reign on earth.

20. HE WILL SEND THEM A SAVIOR: God is to act on behalf of Egypt as He did earlier in delivering Israel (see Judges 2:18; 3:9, 15; 6:7–9; 10:11, 12).

21. KNOW THE LORD IN THAT DAY: The future kingdom will be a time when everyone will know the Lord, because the New Covenant will dominate.

22. STRIKE AND HEAL: Just as a parent disciplines a child for purposes of improvement, so the Lord had dealt and would deal with Egypt.

23. A HIGHWAY FROM EGYPT TO ASSYRIA: The two great warring nations of Isaiah's time are to reach a lasting peace with each other during "that day" of Christ's reign.

24. A BLESSING IN THE MIDST OF THE LAND: Israel "in that day" will become what God intended her to be—a blessing to the world (see Genesis 12:3).

25. MY PEOPLE . . . THE WORK OF MY HANDS: Elsewhere, Scripture uses these epithets to speak only of Israel. However, in the future kingdom, Israel is to be God's instrument for drawing other nations into His fold.

THE SIGN: The Lord God directs the prophet Isaiah to go "naked and barefoot" to serve as a sign of the coming judgment against Egypt and Ethiopia.

20:1. TARTAN: The Hebrew term is probably not a proper name but a title designating a commander in the Assyrian army.

ASHDOD: One of the five largest Philistine cities, all located southwest of Jerusalem.

SARGON: Sargon II, king of Assyria from c. 722–705 BC.

TOOK IT: The Assyrians captured Ashdod in 711 BC, and so frightened the Egyptians that they backed away, thus teaching Judah the folly of reliance on a foreign power for protection.

2. AT THE SAME TIME: Isaiah began his object lesson three years before his speech in verses 3–6, which came just prior to the Assyrian attack in 711 BC.

REMOVE THE SACKCLOTH: This apparel may denote Isaiah's mourning (see Genesis 37:34) or it may signify his prophetic office (see 2 Kings 1:8).

WALKING NAKED AND BAREFOOT: The Lord commanded Isaiah to strip off all of his outer garments as an act denoting disgrace and humiliation.

3. MY SERVANT: This designation places Isaiah among a select group. Others include Abraham, Moses, Caleb, David, Job, Eliakim, the Servant of the Lord, Israel, Zerubbabel, and Christ's followers.

SIGN AND A WONDER: Isaiah's nakedness and bare feet symbolized the coming desolation and shame of Egypt and Ethiopia at the hands of the Assyrians.

4. EGYPTIANS AS PRISONERS ... ETHIOPIANS AS CAPTIVES: Esarhaddon, king of Assyria, fulfilled this prophecy in 671 BC (see 2 Kings 19:37; Ezra 4:2). God was telling the people of Judah that Egypt, far from being a suitable object of their trust, would go off in shame.

6. HOW SHALL WE ESCAPE?: This refers to the people of Judah. Their trust in Egypt will prove to be misplaced.

BACK TO BABYLON: The prophet's declarations again turn to the nation of Babylon.

21:1. WILDERNESS OF THE SEA: The prophet here refers to an area of southern Babylon, near the Persian Gulf, known for its fertility.

AS WHIRLWINDS IN THE SOUTH: The simile is based on the suddenness with which storm winds come from the Negev and sweep through the land of Israel. God is saying that Babylon's overthrown is to be as sudden as those storm winds.

2. GO UP, O ELAM! BESIEGE, O MEDIA: The Elamites and Medes were part of the Persian army that defeated Babylon in 539 BC.

3–4. MY LOINS ARE FILLED WITH PAIN: Isaiah notes here that the severity of the violence about which he must prophesy is causing him extreme agitation.

5. EAT AND DRINK. . . . ANOINT THE SHIELD: This part of the oracle recalls Belshazzar's feast in Daniel 5. Amid the celebration, a call came to fight the attacking enemy invading the city.

6. SET A WATCHMAN: Isaiah stationed a watchman on the city walls.

7. CHARIOT . . . CHARIOT . . . CHARIOT: Isaiah heard the watchman warn of an approaching military force.

8. HE CRIED, "A LION, MY LORD": The Dead Sea Scrolls correctly read, "the watchman cried, my LORD." The watchman whom Isaiah had stationed was continuing his report.

9. BABYLON IS FALLEN, IS FALLEN: The watchman proclaims the tragic end of mighty Babylon, which initially fell to the Assyrians in 689 BC and again to the Persians in 539 BC. Yet Isaiah's prediction here also looks forward to the ultimate fall of the great enemy of God, as verified by John's citation of this verse (see Revelation 14:8; 18:2).

10. MY THRESHING AND THE GRAIN OF MY FLOOR: The violent threshing of grain portrays Babylon's oppression of Israel, and the resultant grain is Israel's deliverance by God. The concise saying offered hope to God's people.

PROPHECY AGAINST EDOM AND ARABIA: Isaiah also issues proclamations from God against the people of Edom and Arabia.

11. DUMAH: This oasis in northern Arabia stood at the intersection of two important routes, one east-west from the Persian Gulf to Petra, and the other north-south between the Red Sea and Tadmor. It was about three hundred miles south of Jerusalem.

SEIR: Another name for Edom, located south of the Dead Sea and the home of Esau's descendants. This is the source of an inquiry directed to Isaiah.

WHAT OF THE NIGHT?: In other words, how long was the Assyrian oppression to last?

12. THE MORNING COMES, AND ALSO THE NIGHT: Isaiah promises a short-lived deliverance from Assyrian oppression, but quickly adds the threat of Babylonian domination to soon follow.

13. IN THE FOREST: The term *thicket*, referring to scrub brush, is a better rendering, given that the land of Arabia has few or no forests.

DEDANITES: Dedan was on the route to the Red Sea, about 290 miles southeast of Dumah, in the northwestern part of the Arabian desert.

14. TEMA: Tema was also on the Red Sea route, about 200 miles southeast of Dumah, in the northwestern part of the Arabian desert.

BRING WATER . . . WITH THEIR BREAD: The prophet indicates that those fleeing the Assyrian army will need supplies.

15. THEY FLED: The interior area of Arabia will be a place of refuge for fugitives fleeing from the sophisticated armament of the Assyrians.

16. GLORY OF KEDAR WILL FAIL: This prophecy anticipated the conquest of the region in the northwestern part of the Arabian desert by Nebuchadnezzar, king of Babylon.

JUDGMENT AGAINST JERUSALEM: God's judgment would not fall solely on Judah's enemies but also on Judah herself. It would even fall on the city of Jerusalem.

22:1. THE VALLEY OF VISION: This refers to Israel, as God often revealed Himself to Jerusalem through visions. However, the unrepentant inhabitants display a marked lack of vision in their oblivion to the destruction that soon awaits them.

WHAT AILS YOU . . . ?: The prophet reproaches the people for celebrating with wild parties when they should have been in deep repentance because of their sins. Apparently, he anticipates a condition that arose in conjunction with Jerusalem's fall to the Babylonians in 586 BC. But similar incursions by the Assyrians in either 711 or 701 BC, from which the Lord delivered the city, had prompted the revelry among the people.

2. NOT SLAIN WITH THE SWORD: Death came as a result of starvation or disease as the Babylonians besieged the city.

3. RULERS HAVE FLED: The leaders, rather than defending the city as they should have done, fled to save their own necks and, in doing so, were captured (see 2 Kings 25:4–7).

4. WEEP BITTERLY: Isaiah's pain is deep. He cannot participate in the revelry, for he sees the reality of the spiritual issues.

5. IT IS A DAY OF TROUBLE: On a former occasion, when the city was about to fall, terror had reigned among the citizens. This was to occur again, leaving no room for merriment.

6. ELAM BORE THE QUIVER . . . KIR UNCOVERED THE SHIELD: These lands had representatives in the Assyrian army that besieged Jerusalem.

7. CHOICEST VALLEYS: Valleys lying both in and around Jerusalem are to be full of enemy troops.

8. HOUSE OF THE FOREST: This structure, constructed by Solomon out of cedars (see 1 Kings 7:2–6), housed weaponry and other valuables (see 1 Kings 10:17; 2 Chronicles 9:20).

9. CITY OF DAVID: Jerusalem bore this name (see 2 Samuel 5:6–7, 9).

LOWER POOL: The pool of Siloam furnished the city's water supply. Hezekiah's lengthy underground conduit fed the pool from the Gihon Spring.

10. FORTIFY THE WALL: Hezekiah rebuilt the damaged wall, but he did so while trusting God. His faith contrasts with that of the people whom Isaiah currently addresses.

11. OLD POOL: This refers to the Gihon Spring, which the prophet sometimes refers to as the "upper pool" (see Isaiah 7:3; 36:2).

DID NOT LOOK TO ITS MAKER: The preparations made for the city's defense were purely external. The people gave no thought to the Creator of the city, the pool, or the present crisis, against whom their physical defenses were useless.

12: INSTEAD, JOY AND GLADNESS: In the face of a crisis that requires genuine repentance, the people respond with hilarity and self-indulgence. This spirit contrasts with the legitimate joy and gladness of God's people that is later seen in Isaiah 35:10 and 51:11.

13. LET US EAT AND DRINK, FOR TOMORROW WE DIE: Paul cites this same philosophy: "If the dead do not rise, 'Let us eat and drink, for tomorrow we die!'" (1 Corinthians 15:32). If there is no resurrection, enjoyment in this life is all that matters. This worldview utterly disregards God's eternal values.

14. NO ATONEMENT: The Lord's prediction about the outcome of Isaiah's ministry (see 6:9–10) found fulfillment.

15. SHEBNA, WHO IS OVER THE HOUSE: This man, possibly of Egyptian extraction, was second in authority only to the king. Other Old Testament citations refer to him as a scribe (see 2 Kings 18:37; 19:2), which was his position after his demotion from steward, as prophesied by Isaiah.

16. HEWN A SEPULCHER: Shebna arranged for the construction of a tomb fit for a king as a memorial for himself, when he should have been attending to the spiritual affairs of Judah. The prophet condemns his arrogance.

17. MIGHTY MAN: Isaiah again refers to Shebna's glorious estimate of himself.

18. THERE YOU SHALL DIE: Sheba, far from receiving a luxurious burial in Jerusalem, died a shameful death in a foreign country.

19. DRIVE YOU OUT OF YOUR OFFICE: Arrogance caused Shebna's demotion from steward to scribe some time later in Hezekiah's reign, but before 701 BC.

20. MY SERVANT ELIAKIM: Eliakim, who replaced Shebna as steward or prime minister, was highly honored in being called "My servant" by the Lord.

21. A FATHER TO THE INHABITANTS OF JERUSALEM: The steward had supreme authority under the king's oversight.

22. KEY OF THE HOUSE OF DAVID: This authority to admit or refuse admittance into the king's presence evidenced the king's great confidence in Eliakim. Jesus later applied this terminology to Himself as one who could determine who would enter His future Davidic kingdom. "These things says He who is holy, He who is true, 'He who has the key of David, He who opens and no one shuts, and shuts and no one opens'" (Revelation 3:7).

23–25. A GLORIOUS THRONE: This symbolizes the honor Eliakim was to bring to his family. But Eliakim would falter and fall after a time of faithful service, and all those who were "hanging" on him would fall as well.

UNLEASHING THE TEXT

1) Which of the nations and territories mentioned in these chapters do you recognize from the modern world?

_____

_____

_____

_____

2) How can you determine which of these prophecies have already been fulfilled and which are yet to come?

_____

_____

_____

_____

_____

3) What did God command Isaiah to do in chapter 20? What was the intended purpose?

_____

_____

_____

_____

_____

4) How had Jerusalem rebelled against God as described in Isaiah 22?

_____

_____

_____

_____

_____

EXPLORING THE MEANING

Many biblical prophecies have yet to be fulfilled. There is potential for confusion when it comes to understanding and engaging biblical prophecies, and much of that confusion can be connected to the timelines involved. After all, many prophecies that addressed the future to the people of Isaiah's day actually point to events that occurred long ago to modern readers. These include the conquest of Israel, the destruction of Jerusalem, the birth of Jesus, and more.

However, it's important to remember that many of Isaiah's prophetic proclamations have *yet* to be fulfilled. They point to a moment in history that is still the future even for modern readers. We see one such example in Isaiah 19, where the prophet writes, "In that day there will be an altar to the LORD in the midst of the land of Egypt, and a pillar to the LORD at its border. And it will be for a sign and for a witness to the LORD of hosts in the land of Egypt; for they will cry to the LORD because of the oppressors, and He will send them a Savior and a Mighty One, and He will deliver them" (verses 19–20).

This passage from Isaiah describes a future moment in time, when large portions of Egypt will actually align with Judah in worshiping the one true God. In Isaiah's day, such a dramatic turn in Egypt's spiritual condition would have been unthinkable. Even today, with the political realities of our world, such spiritual unity seems unlikely. However, Isaiah tells us that Egyptian citizens will one day speak "the language of Canaan" (verse 18) as they worship the Lord! We can look forward in faith to that future time and the further affirmation of the inerrancy and authority of God's Word.

God goes to great lengths to speak with humanity. There is a moment in Isaiah 20 that can come across as genuinely surprising—perhaps even shocking— to modern readers. As the prophet writes, "At the same time the LORD spoke by Isaiah the son of Amoz, saying, 'Go, and remove the sackcloth from your body, and take your sandals off your feet.' And he did so, walking naked and barefoot" (verse 2). Isaiah was commanded to walk around naked *for three years* to illustrate the coming judgment against Egypt and Ethiopia, in which both countries would experience captivity and hardship for three years.

This might sound like an extreme way to make a point. However, the reality is that throughout Scripture, God often uses extreme measures to get people's attention. For example, God commanded Hosea, another prophet, to marry an unfaithful woman as an illustration of Israel's spiritual adultery (see Hosea 1:2). He commanded the prophet Ezekiel to lie on his side for 390 days and eat bread baked over cow dung to warn the nation of Israel about God's coming judgment. He commanded Jeremiah to buy a field when his country was overrun by Babylonian invaders and everyone else was converting their land into cash and valuables.

Of course, the most striking method God has used to capture the attention of humanity was the Incarnation—including the birth, life, ministry, death, and resurrection of Jesus Christ. As John writes, "The Word became flesh and dwelt among us" (John 1:14). Through Jesus, God took on human nature and a body of flesh to offer Himself as a perfect sacrifice so that the penalty for our sins could be paid and our relationship with God could be restored.

We are stewards of God's blessings. As mentioned earlier, Isaiah 22 is a surprising chapter because it speaks of judgment not against a foreign nation such as Babylon or Ethiopia, but against Judah—even Jerusalem itself. In the middle of that proclamation of judgment, however, Isaiah stops to highlight a specific individual: "Thus says the Lord GOD of hosts: 'Go, proceed to this steward, to Shebna, who is over the house, and say: "What have you here, and whom have you here, that you have hewn a sepulcher here, as he who hews himself a sepulcher on high, who carves a tomb for himself in a rock?"'" (verses 15–16).

Shebna was the steward over Jerusalem, which meant he had been entrusted with a high degree of authority and power. Perhaps he was even second in command to the king. Apparently, Shebna had created a huge tomb in his own honor, similar to the kings of Egypt. God used this tomb as an illustration not only of *Shebna's* poor stewardship but also of the poor stewardship of the people in Judah more generally. The scene that Isaiah paints in chapter 22 is of a people dancing and singing in a raucous party even as the Babylonian army begins laying the siege that would destroy the city.

In a similar way, Christians today must recognize that we are stewards of the blessings God has given us. Those blessings include our resources—time, treasure, talents—but also the blessings of Scripture and the presence of the Holy Spirit. We have been given those blessings for a *purpose*. We have work to do.

REFLECTING ON THE TEXT

5) How does fulfilled prophecy build your confidence in the inerrancy and authority of God's Word?

_____

_____

_____

_____

_____

_____

6) What should we take away from the shocking imagery that God's Word uses to describe sin and its consequences?

_____

_____

_____

_____

_____

7) What specific blessings and privileges do you enjoy in Christ?

_____

_____

_____

_____

_____

8) Are you currently a faithful or an unfaithful steward of the blessings you have received from God? Explain.

_____

_____

_____

_____

_____

PERSONAL RESPONSE

9) Considering the great lengths God has gone to in communicating and preserving His Word, how should we respond?

_____

_____

_____

_____

_____

10) What steps can you take this week to more seriously consider your role as a steward of God's blessings?

_____

_____

_____

_____

_____

_____

_____

5

REDEMPTION OF ISRAEL

Isaiah 24:1–27:13

DRAWING NEAR

How do you typically respond when people claim the end of the world is near?

_____

_____

_____

_____

_____

_____

_____

_____

_____

_____

THE CONTEXT

As we've seen in previous lessons, Isaiah 13–23 offers proclamations of God's coming judgment against many nations of the ancient world. In many cases, powerful nations such as Assyria and Babylon were used as the instruments of that judgment. They swept across the land, bringing conquest and destruction in their wake. However, God subsequently also judged those nations. No nation was large enough or strong enough to escape the consequences of their actions.

Isaiah 24 is in many ways the culmination of these prophetic judgments. In this portion of Isaiah's vision, he sees the entire earth devasted, ruined, and broken down as a result of God's wrath. This picture looks ahead to the day of judgment at the end of history.

From there, Isaiah's prophecy takes an interesting and perhaps unexpected turn. In Isaiah 25–27, we find expressions of praise for the ways in which God will bring about redemption and salvation for His people. This redemption is specifically focused on the future of the Israelites but it also points to the ultimate redemption for all of God's people through the death and resurrection of Jesus Christ.

KEYS TO THE TEXT

Read Isaiah 24:1–27:13, noting the key words and phrases indicated below.

> *JUDGMENT AGAINST TYRE: The proclamations from God continue, here focusing on the prosperous seaport of Tyre.*

23:1. TYRE: A Phoenician seaport on the Mediterranean Sea, located about thirty-five miles north of Mount Carmel and twenty-eight miles west of Mount Hermon. Tyre supplied lumber for King Solomon's temple and sailors for his navy (see 1 Kings 5:1, 7–12; 9:26–27).

YOU SHIPS OF TARSHISH: Tarshish was most likely located in Spain, which means that "ships of Tarshish" were large trading vessels capable of making distant voyages on the open sea, all the way to the port of Tyre.

LAID WASTE: Tyre was under siege five times between when this prophecy was given and 332 BC. Only the last of these attacks (by Alexander the Great, in 332 BC) would completely level and subdue the city. Ezekiel prophesied this destruction (see Ezekiel 26:3–27:36).

NO HOUSE, NO HARBOR: Sailors, weary from their long and difficult journey, would find no customary haven of rest upon arrival at their destination in Tyre.

CYPRUS: Sailors would learn of Tyre's overthrow when they reached this island located in the eastern Mediterranean.

2. SIDON: Sidon was the other important Phoenician seaport, along with Tyre. Here, it represents the rest of Phoenicia's response to Tyre's overthrow.

3. GRAIN OF SHIHOR: The Phoenicians carried grain grown in Egypt (represented by Shihor) aboard their ships. They also bought and sold much of the commodity.

4. I DO NOT LABOR, NOR BRING FORTH CHILDREN: Isaiah frequently speaks of barrenness, labor, and childbirth (see, for example, 7:14; 8:3; 9:6; 26:16–18; 37:3). Here, the figure describes Tyre, "the strength of the sea," bemoaning her desolate condition.

6–7. TARSHISH . . . FAR OFF TO DWELL: Tyre's refugees would travel throughout the Mediterranean world (see verse 1). They, too, lament the city's fall.

8. THE CROWNING CITY . . . PRINCES . . . HONORABLE: Tyre was a very old city, dating from about two millennia before Christ. The city had high international prestige.

9. THE PRIDE OF ALL GLORY: This provides the reason why the Lord of Hosts will bring the overthrow of Tyre—their foolish arrogance stemming from the city's prestige.

10. NO MORE STRENGTH: The oracle invites the colonies of Tyre to exercise their freedom in taking advantage of the city's fall.

11. THE LORD HAS GIVEN A COMMANDMENT AGAINST CANAAN: The Lord had caused the downfall of the territory of Canaan, which included Tyre and Sidon.

12. VIRGIN DAUGHTER OF SIDON: The city of Sidon, once noted for its freshness and revelry, will become like a used-up old woman, piecing together what is left. God used the Assyrians to crush her (contrast the virgin daughter of Zion in Isaiah 37:22).

13. LAND OF THE CHALDEANS . . . WILD BEASTS OF THE DESERT: The example of the Chaldeans (another name for the Babylonians) reminded the people of Tyre of their hopelessness against the forces of Assyria, which ravaged Babylon in 689 BC.

15. FORGOTTEN SEVENTY YEARS: Alexander the Great would destroy Tyre, but the devastation would not be permanent. A little village remains on the site of the ancient city to this present day. (The timeframe of the seventy years is obscure, possibly dating c. 700–630 BC.)

15. IN THE SONG OF THE HARLOT: Harlots sang to draw attention to themselves—attention that was not so hard to obtain in ancient days. Like those harlots, the people of Tyre are invited to sing songs drawing attention to their earlier prosperity.

17. THE LORD WILL DEAL: With God's help, the city was to return.

18. SET APART FOR THE LORD: Even Tyre's sinful gain was to support Judah as her colonies once supported her.

JUDGMENT ON THE EARTH: Moving beyond national borders, Isaiah now speaks of a day when the entire earth will bear the brunt of God's wrath.

24:1. THE LORD MAKES THE EARTH EMPTY: In this next section (through Isaiah 27:13), the prophet generalizes and broadens the destruction about which he had written specifically in Isaiah 13–23. The Lord is to deal with the whole earth more severely than He did at the Tower of Babel or through the Great Flood.

2. AS WITH THE PEOPLE, SO WITH THE PRIEST: Neither rank, wealth, nor power is able to deliver from God's judgment.

3. THE LORD HAS SPOKEN: Isaiah used this expression (or one comparable) nine other times to emphasize the certainty of his predictions (see Isaiah 1:20; 21:17; 22:25; 25:8; 37:22; 38:7; 38:15; 40:5; 58:14).

4. HAUGHTY PEOPLE OF THE EARTH: The prophet again calls attention to pride as the reason for God's judgment. "Everyone proud in heart is an abomination to the LORD; though they join forces, none will go unpunished" (Proverbs 16:5).

5. BROKEN THE EVERLASTING COVENANT: Most likely this refers to the Abrahamic covenant, which in the Old Testament is frequently spoken of as "everlasting" (see, for example, Genesis 17:7, 13, 19; 1 Chronicles 16:15, 17; Psalms 105:8, 10).

6. THE INHABITANTS OF THE EARTH ARE BURNED . . . FEW MEN ARE LEFT: This Gentile remnant differs from that of Israel. Presumably, they will join in support of Israel when the Messiah returns.

7. ALL THE MERRY-HEARTED SIGH: The future day of judgment will terminate all merriment derived from natural sources. "The sound of harpists, musicians, flutists, and trumpeters shall not be heard in you anymore. No craftsman of any craft shall be found in you anymore, and the sound of a millstone shall not be heard in you anymore" (Revelation 18:22).

10. EVERY HOUSE IS SHUT UP: Houses normally provided security from outside harm, but they now became inaccessible.

13. SHAKING OF AN OLIVE TREE: The same figure spoke of leanness in the judgment against Ephraim in Isaiah 17:6.

14. THEY SHALL LIFT UP THEIR VOICE: The songs of the godly remnant (see verse 6), celebrating God's righteous judgment, replace the drunken music (see verse 9).

15. GLORIFY THE LORD: This call summons all people worldwide to attribute to the Lord what is due Him.

16. GLORY TO THE RIGHTEOUS: "Righteous" in this verse refers to God.

BUT I: Isaiah could not yet join in the celebration of God's glory because he was pondering the grief and corruption in the world before that final celebration of God's victory.

17. THE PIT AND THE SNARE: The figure of an animal caught in a trap set by humans frequently symbolized the principle that life is a series of inescapable traps (see, for example, 2 Samuel 22:6; Job 18:8–10; 22:10; Psalms 18:5; 64:5; 106:36; 124:7).

18. WINDOWS FROM ON HIGH: In Noah's day, God judged the earth with a flood (see Genesis 7:11). He will judge again from heaven, but this time not with a flood (see Revelation 6:13–14; 8:3–13; 16:1–21). Unparalleled earthquakes will mark the future visitation, during and after the fulfillment of Daniel's seventieth-week prophecy.

20. LIKE A DRUNKARD . . . LIKE A HUT: These two illustrations—a staggering drunkard and a flimsy lean-to hut—picture the ultimate collapse of the presumably strong and dependable planet earth.

21. THE LORD WILL PUNISH ON HIGH: In the climactic phase of the Day of the Lord, He will strike against rebelling forces, both angelic and human.

22. SHUT UP IN THE PRISON: The New Testament authors wrote more about the imprisonment of fallen angels before their final assignment to the lake of fire (see 2 Peter 2:4; Jude 6; Revelation 9:2, 3, 11; 20:1–10) and likewise revealed more regarding the fate of unbelieving humans (Luke 16:19–31; Revelation 20:11–15).

23. THE MOON WILL BE DISGRACED . . . THE SUN ASHAMED: In the eternal state after Christ's millennial reign, the glory of God and of the Lamb will replace the sun and moon as sources of light. "The city had no need of the sun or of the moon to shine in it, for the glory of God illuminated it. The Lamb is its light" (Revelation 21:23).

REIGN . . . IN JERUSALEM: John later confirmed this clear prophecy of the Messiah's future earthly reign in Jerusalem (see Revelation 11:15–17; 19:6, 16).

> THE BLESSING OF SALVATION: *Judgment is not the only focus of Isaiah's prophecies. In this passage, the prophet speaks about God's plan for salvation.*

25:1. YOU HAVE DONE WONDERFUL THINGS: Isaiah responds to God's final judgment of the world with praise to Him for planning His actions long before their implementation.

2. A CITY A RUIN . . . NEVER BE REBUILT: Isaiah does not stipulate which city, but a prophecy of Babylon's final destruction is in keeping with the context (see Isaiah 21:9).

3. STRONG PEOPLE . . . TERRIBLE NATIONS: When Christ reigns on earth, nations from the whole world will glorify and fear Him (see Isaiah 24:14–16).

4. YOU HAVE BEEN A STRENGTH TO THE POOR: Another indicator of God's worthiness to be glorified is His upholding of the oppressed.

5. AS HEAT IN A DRY PLACE . . . STORM: These two weather extremes in Judah's climate—the sudden thunderstorm and the relentless heat—illustrate how God will harbor the poor and needy.

6. THIS MOUNTAIN: In God's eternal kingdom, the Lord will host His great banquet on Mount Zion for the faithful remnant.

7. THE COVERING CAST OVER ALL PEOPLE: God will remove the death shrouds from those in attendance at His banquet.

8. SWALLOW UP DEATH: God will swallow up death, which itself functions as a swallower of human beings. "Let us swallow them alive like Sheol, and whole, like those who go down to the Pit" (Proverbs 1:12). Paul later noted the fulfillment of this promise in the resurrection of believers when he wrote, "So when this corruptible has put on incorruption, and this mortal has put on immortality, then shall be brought to pass the saying that is written: 'Death is swallowed up in victory'" (1 Corinthians 15:54).

THE LORD GOD WILL WIPE AWAY TEARS: God will remove the sorrow associated with death. John would later allude to the tender action of this verse to describe the bliss of the redeemed in heaven (see Revelation 7:17) and the ideal conditions in the New Jerusalem (see 21:4).

THE REBUKE OF HIS PEOPLE HE WILL TAKE AWAY: Israel will be the head of the nations and no longer the tail (see Deuteronomy 28:13).

9. WE HAVE WAITED FOR HIM: To wait for God involves an ultimate trust in Him, not becoming impatient when His timetable for final salvation differs from one's own expectations.

10. MOAB: Moab represents the rest of the nations, as does Edom elsewhere.

12. THE FORTRESS OF THE HIGH FORT: Moabite cities had highly fortified and elevated walls. Yet not even these will withstand God's judgment.

A SONG OF SALVATION: Isaiah relates the song of praise that the redeemed remnant "in that day" will sing to God over Jerusalem, their impregnable city.

26:1. STRONG CITY: In contrast to the typical city of confusion that was doomed (see Isaiah 24:10; 25:2; 26:5), God has a future city of prominence—the millennial Jerusalem. As Zechariah would later write, "The people shall dwell in it; and no longer shall there be utter destruction, but Jerusalem shall be safely inhabited" (Zechariah 14:11).

2. OPEN THE GATES: Isaiah envisions the future Jerusalem, where only righteous Israel may enter. The redeemed remnant from other nations will come there periodically to worship.

3. YOU WILL KEEP HIM IN PERFECT PEACE: A fixed disposition of trust in the Lord brings a peace that the wicked can never know. Such reliance precludes doublemindedness (see James 1:6–8) and serving two masters (see Matthew 6:24).

4. EVERLASTING STRENGTH: Literally, this expression is "Rock of Ages," referring to a rocky cliff where the trusting person may find shelter from attackers.

5. HE BRINGS DOWN THOSE WHO DWELL ON HIGH: The arrogant inhabit the lofty city during its overthrow, but the humble inhabit the strong city during its later exaltation.

7. UPRIGHTNESS . . . WEIGH: The Hebrew word translated "uprightness" means "straight," and the meaning of "weigh" is "make level." Isaiah is speaking here of a straight and level path for the feet of the poor and needy in a land filled with hilly and twisting roads.

8. WE HAVE WAITED FOR YOU: Isaiah divulges the key to the redemption of the future remnant—their dependence on the Lord, not humanly devised schemes.

9. DESIRED YOU IN THE NIGHT . . . WILL SEEK YOU EARLY: The pious long for God at all times.

WILL LEARN RIGHTEOUSNESS: God's punishing hand benefits sinners in leading them to repentance.

10. NOT LEARN RIGHTEOUSNESS: God shows His love and mercy toward other wicked people, but they turn their back on it.

11. THEY WILL NOT SEE: The wicked, who are blind to God's authority and imminent judgment, will be conscious of His compassion for His people Israel—to their own shame.

12. YOU WILL ESTABLISH PEACE: Although Israel's immediate future looks bleak, Isaiah expresses strong confidence that the nation will ultimately prosper.

13. MASTERS BESIDES YOU: Israel's history was replete with periods of foreign domination by the likes of Egypt and Assyria.

14. THEY WILL NOT RISE: These foreign overlords are to be a thing of the past. They are not to appear again on the earthly scene.

15. HAVE INCREASED THE NATION: Isaiah, with prophetic certainty from the perspective of Israel's future restoration, saw the expansion of Israel's borders as an accomplished fact.

16. YOUR CHASTENING WAS UPON THEM: The hard experiences of Israel's history drove her to call on God.

17–18. AS A WOMAN WITH CHILD: Israel's tumultuous history is here compared to a pregnant woman in labor.

18. NOT ACCOMPLISHED ANY DELIVERANCE: All the nation's effort was to no avail, because they did not depend on the Lord.

19. DEAD SHALL LIVE: This speaks of the raising of corporate Israel to participate in the great future banquet (see Ezekiel 37).

THE RESTORATION OF ISRAEL: *The coming day of the Lord will include the restoration of His chosen people and their promised land.*

20. FOR A LITTLE MOMENT: Israel's final restoration was not immediately at hand. For this reason, the people had to continue praying in solitude for that restoration, until the time of God's indignation would pass.

21. DISCLOSE HER BLOOD: The innocent killed by their oppressors are to come to life (see verse 19) and testify against their murderers.

27:2. A VINEYARD OF RED WINE: This vineyard is Israel and contrasts sharply with the one depicted in Isaiah 5:1–7. Far from a disappointment to the vinekeeper, this one bore abundant fruit (see 27:6).

3. I KEEP IT NIGHT AND DAY: God's future provisions for restored Israel will be complete.

4. FURY IS NOT IN ME: The time for Israel's punishment by God will pass.

5. MAKE PEACE WITH ME: The enemies of Israel may make peace with God.

6. THE FACE OF THE WORLD: In the future kingdom of the Messiah, restored Israel will rule with Him and fill the earth with the fruit of righteousness and peace.

7. STRUCK ISRAEL AS HE STRUCK: God has tempered His dealings with Israel, but not so with those He used to punish Israel. His compassion for the other nations has come to an end.

8. SENDING IT AWAY: The Lord sent Judah into captivity to awaken the nation's trust in Him.

9. INIQUITY OF JACOB WILL BE COVERED: Jacob atoned for his iniquity by undergoing punishment from God.

10. WILL BE DESOLATE: This city symbolizes Judah's oppressors.

11. WILL NOT HAVE MERCY ON THEM: In contrast with His dealings with Israel, the Creator will deal a fatal blow to her enemies.

12. GATHERED ONE BY ONE: After the judgment of Israel's enemies at the end of Daniel's seventieth week, the faithful remnant of Israelites will return to their land (see Matthew 24:31).

13. WORSHIP THE LORD . . . AT JERUSALEM: The prophet here reiterates one of his great themes: future worship of regathered Israel on Mount Zion (see Isaiah 24:23; 25:6–7, 10).

UNLEASHING THE TEXT

1) What have you been taught about the judgment awaiting our world at the end of history?

_____

_____

_____

_____

2) Why is Isaiah's praise in chapter 25 an appropriate response to the judgment predicted in chapter 24?

_____

_____

_____

_____

_____

3) What images catch your attention from Isaiah 26? What do those images communicate?

_____

_____

_____

_____

_____

4) Isaiah 27 describes the restoration of Israel. Why is that good news for the church?

_____

_____

_____

_____

_____

EXPLORING THE MEANING

This world is not our home. One of the themes emphasized throughout Isaiah's prophecy is the coming Day of the Lord, when God's judgment will fully fall upon the earth and its inhabitants. Part of that judgment will include the destruction of our planet. In Isaiah's words:

> The earth is violently broken,
> The earth is split open,
> The earth is shaken exceedingly.
> The earth shall reel to and fro like a drunkard,
> And shall totter like a hut;

Its transgression shall be heavy upon it,
And it will fall, and not rise again (24:19–20).

As we've seen, the Day of the Lord is a theme revisited many times throughout Scripture. For instance, the prophet Joel wrote, "The sun shall be turned into darkness, and the moon into blood, before the coming of the great and awesome day of the LORD" (2:31). Peter added, "But the day of the Lord will come as a thief in the night, in which the heavens will pass away with a great noise, and the elements will melt with fervent heat; both the earth and the works that are in it will be burned up" (2 Peter 3:10).

Ultimately, however, this destruction will lay the groundwork for something wonderful: a new earth devoid of the corruption of sin. This world is not our home; it is a stopping place. Our actual home will be an eternal paradise. John received a vision of this new home, which caused him to write these words to the church: "I saw a new heaven and a new earth, for the first heaven and the first earth had passed away. . . . [There] God will wipe away every tear from their eyes; there shall be no more death, nor sorrow, nor crying. There shall be no more pain, for the former things have passed away" (Revelation 21:1, 4).

God is worthy of our trust. The theme of judgment is unpleasant—purposefully so—which is one of the reasons God's prophets were despised in their own times. Many were even put to death. However, the reality of future judgment does not need to be a cause of angst or distress for God's people. Why? Because the reality of future judgment is yet another reminder that God is in control.

Just as important, God's sovereignty over nations—both past and future—reminds us that God is worthy of our trust. The judgments prophesied in Isaiah, and elsewhere in Scripture, are not random events capable of springing upon humanity at any time. Instead, they are a measured and ordered part of God's larger plan of redemption—a plan we can trust.

Isaiah touched on this issue of trust in chapter 26 when he wrote, "You will keep him in perfect peace, whose mind is stayed on You, because he trusts in You. Trust in the LORD forever, for in YAH, the LORD, is everlasting strength" (verses 3–4). We serve a God who holds not just our world in His hand, but also the entire universe. As such, we can trust Him to manage the ins and outs and everyday details of our lives.

Israel will be restored. Another theme that occurs throughout Isaiah's prophecy is the future restoration of Israel, both as a nation and as God's chosen people. "In that day sing to her, 'A vineyard of red wine! I, the LORD, keep it, I water it every moment; lest any hurt it, I keep it night and day'" (Isaiah 27:2–3). In Scripture, the image of a vineyard represents Israel. Here, Isaiah reminds his hearers that God will continue to tend and cherish that vineyard, even through the seasons of judgment already described.

Later, Isaiah proclaimed, "Those who come He shall cause to take root in Jacob; Israel shall blossom and bud, and fill the face of the world with fruit" (verse 6). The prophet was describing a moment when God's people would no longer be scattered throughout the earth, but would return to the promised land. The initial fulfillment of that promise occurred in 1948, when the nation of Israel was reestablished after the horrors of World War II. This was unprecedented; Israel had been disbanded as a nation for more than fifteen centuries. Yet its return was prophesied by Isaiah more than seven centuries before the birth of Christ.

Beyond a physical nation, however, Isaiah's prophecy reminds us that God will not abandon His chosen people, Israel. And, one day, those same people will turn back to God and worship Him.

REFLECTING ON THE TEXT

5) If you are a Christian, this world is not your real home. What impact does the fact have on your actions?

_____

_____

_____

_____

6) Scripture is clear about the future destruction of earth and God's final judgement of sin. What should you do in light of those forthcoming events?

_____

_____

_____

_____

7) What does it mean to trust God?

8) How should the church view and interact with the Jewish people today?

PERSONAL RESPONSE

9) What are some specific ways you can cultivate the mindset that this world is not your home and act accordingly?

10) Where do you have an opportunity this week to actively and intentionally exercise your trust in God?

6

WARNINGS AGAINST
ALLIANCE WITH EGYPT
Isaiah 28:1–30:33; 35:1–10

DRAWING NEAR
What are some of the biggest sources of distraction in your life?

_____

_____

_____

_____

_____

_____

_____

_____

THE CONTEXT
As mentioned previously, one of the difficulties in engaging and understanding the prophetic books in Scripture is the way they often swing back and forth between different periods of time. We will encounter one of those swings in this next section of Isaiah. In the previous lesson, we saw how Isaiah's focus shifted away from the judgment of the nations surrounding God's people and looked forward to the day of Israel's redemption and restoration.

In this lesson, we will watch as Isaiah swings his attention back to the present moment of his hearers. Specifically, Isaiah focuses on the threat Assyria poses to Israel and Judah. Much of the chapters under discussion focus on the failure of leadership in both Israel and Judah. Kings and courtesans were busy intoxicating themselves with wine, and in many ways they were oblivious to the threat Assyria posed until its armies were at their door. Isaiah 30–31 condemn Judah's leaders for considering Egypt their source of rescue rather than God.

As we will see, Isaiah again accurately foretold the coming destruction of Israel at Assyria's hands. He also correctly prophesied that Assyria would besiege Jerusalem—yet not destroy it. We will also see God's promise of judgment against Assyria and Babylon, along with another glimpse of the future glory of Zion.

KEYS TO THE TEXT

Read Isaiah 28:1–30:33, noting the key words and phrases indicated below.

> *A PICTURE OF POOR LEADERSHIP: Isaiah declares "woe" on Israel and Judah because of the many poor decisions their leaders will make.*

28:1. WOE TO THE CROWN: The prominent thought is impending disaster. The "crown of pride" refers to Samaria, whose walls were the "crown" of a beautiful hill that overlooked a lush valley leading toward the Mediterranean coast.

EPHRAIM: The northern kingdom of Israel had fallen to the Assyrians, leaving a lesson for Jerusalem, under similar circumstances, to learn about foreign alliances.

2. A FLOOD OF MIGHTY WATERS: Isaiah here draws on forceful figures of speech to wake his readers from their lethargy in the face of an impending Assyrian invasion.

4. FIRST FRUIT BEFORE THE SUMMER: Figs that ripened before the end-of-summer harvest were devoured immediately. The Assyrian conquest of Ephraim would be just as rapid.

5. CROWN OF GLORY: The true crown will replace the fraudulent "crown of pride."

6. SPIRIT OF JUSTICE: In the day of the Messiah's reign, the empowering Spirit will prevail in bringing justice to the world (see Isaiah 11:2).

7. THE PRIEST AND THE PROPHET HAVE ERRED: Drunkenness had infected even the religious leadership of the nation, resulting in false spiritual guidance of the people.

8. NO PLACE IS CLEAN: When leaders wallow in filth, what hope does a nation have?

9. WEANED FROM MILK: The drunken leaders resented it when Isaiah and true prophets treated them as toddlers by reminding them of elementary truths of right and wrong.

10. PRECEPT MUST BE UPON PRECEPT, PRECEPT UPON PRECEPT: This is the drunkard's sarcastically mocking response to corrective advice from the prophet. The Hebrew monosyllables in this verse imitate a young child's babbling ridicule of Isaiah's preaching.

11. ANOTHER TONGUE: The drunkards refuse to listen to God's prophet, so they will become subservient to Assyrian taskmasters who will command them in a foreign language.

12. THIS IS THE REST . . . THE REFRESHING . . . THEY WOULD NOT HEAR: The Lord, in simple language they could understand, offered them relief from their oppressors, but they would not listen.

13. PRECEPT UPON PRECEPT: In light of their rejection, the Lord imitates the mockery of the drunkards in jabber they could not understand.

14. HEAR THE WORD OF THE LORD: In light of the tragedies that had befallen Ephraim, the scornful leaders in Jerusalem needed to steer a course different from relying on foreign powers.

15. COVENANT WITH DEATH: The scornful leaders in Jerusalem had made an agreement with Egypt to help defend themselves against the Assyrians. They had yielded to expediency for the sake of security and, without admitting it, had taken refuge in deceit and falsehood.

> A SURE FOUNDATION: *The Lord contrasts the only sure refuge found in Him with the false refuge of relying on foreigners. This points to the coming of the Messiah.*

16. WILL NOT ACT HASTILY: The Greek Old Testament interprets this Hebrew verb for "hurry" in the sense of "put to shame," furnishing the basis of the New Testament citations of this verse (see Romans 9:33; 10:11; 1 Peter 2:6).

17. JUSTICE THE MEASURING LINE: When the Messiah rules His kingdom, the system of justice will contrast strongly with the refuge of lies in which Jerusalem's leaders are engaged.

18. COVENANT WITH DEATH . . . WILL NOT STAND: Trusting in foreign deliverers will utterly fail.

19. MORNING BY MORNING: The Assyrians will repeatedly plunder the area around Jerusalem, provoking great terror among the city's inhabitants.

20. BED IS TOO SHORT . . . COVERING SO NARROW: A proverbial expression about short beds and narrow sheets, telling Jerusalem that foreign alliances are inadequate to defend the city.

21. MOUNT PERAZIM . . . VALLEY OF GIBEON: Just as the Lord defeated the Philistines at Mount Perazim (see 2 Samuel 5:19–20), and the Canaanites in the Valley of Gibeon (see Joshua 10:6–11), so He will do against any who mock Him, even Jerusalemites.

22. DESTRUCTION DETERMINED: God has decreed something unusual—the destruction of His own wicked people. Yet they can still escape if they repent.

23. GIVE EAR: The next section of Isaiah's prophecy draws on the imagery of a farmer as a parable to show how God deals with His people. As the farmer does his different tasks, each in the right season and proportion, so God adopts His measures to His purposes—now mercy, then judgment; punishing sooner, then later. His purpose is not to destroy His people, any more than the farmer's object in his threshing or plowing is to destroy his crop.

24. KEEP PLOWING . . . KEEP TURNING: No ordinary farmer plows and turns the soil endlessly. He sows in accord with what is proper.

25. SOW . . . SCATTER . . . PLANT: After preparing the soil, the farmer carefully plants the seed.

26. GOD TEACHES HIM: Farming intelligently is a God-given instinct.

29. EXCELLENT IN GUIDANCE: Just as God's way in the physical realm of farming is best, so His way is also best in spiritual matters.

WOE TO JERUSALEM: Isaiah turns to prophesying a "woe" against the city of Jerusalem because of her unfaithfulness to the Lord. But he also states that those who cause the city's destruction will face judgment.

29:1 ARIEL: The word means "lion of God," referring to the city's strength, and perhaps "hearth of God," referring to the place where the altar of God always burns. The chapter looks to the invasion of Jerusalem because of the people's unbelief.

WHERE DAVID DWELT: David named Jerusalem "the city of David."

FEASTS: Jerusalem's cycle of religious ceremonies was meaningless to God.

3. LAY SIEGE: God encamped against Jerusalem through His instruments, first the Assyrians (701 BC) and then the Babylonians (586 BC).

4. OUT OF THE DUST: Jerusalem will be like a captive, humbled in the dust. Her voice will come from the earth like that of a medium spirit—like the voice of the dead was supposed to be. This would be fitting for her sins of necromancy.

5–8. THE MULTITUDE OF YOUR FOES: However, in God's time, after Jerusalem's punishment, those who fought against the city will themselves come under God's judgment.

6. THUNDER AND EARTHQUAKE AND GREAT NOISE: This terminology points to the storm theophany marking the termination of the seals, trumpets, and bowls in Revelation (see Revelation 8:5; 11:19; 16:18).

7. AS A DREAM: All the threats to the city from enemy nations will fade like a bad dream.

8. EMPTY . . . FAINT: Jerusalem's attackers will frustrate themselves, like a dreamer who has the illusion that he eats and drinks but awakens to find himself still hungry and thirsty.

> THE BLIND: *The prophet now returns to the theme of the spiritual blindness and mechanical religion that is not pleasing to God.*

9. BLIND . . . DRUNK: The blindness and drunkenness came from the people's inability to comprehend Isaiah's message about trusting God instead of Egypt.

10. SPIRIT OF DEEP SLEEP: Israel refused to hear God's true prophets, so He gave them up judicially to their own hardness of heart. Paul later applied this verse specifically to the general condition of Israel's blindness during the age of the church (see Romans 11:8).

11. ONE WHO IS LITERATE: Those with ability to read and have "the whole vision" could not do so because they had surrendered their spiritual sensitivity.

12. ONE WHO IS ILLITERATE: The uneducated had two reasons for not knowing this vision: (1) the book was sealed, and (2) even if it were not, they would not be able to read it. It is deplorable when *no one* is capable of receiving God's rich revelation.

13. REMOVED THEIR HEARTS FAR FROM ME: Empty ritualism does not bring closeness to God.

14. WISDOM . . . PERISH . . . UNDERSTANDING . . . HIDDEN: The spiritual plague of Jerusalem was the people's reliance on human wisdom rather than divine wisdom.

15. HIDE THEIR COUNSEL: Isaiah is likely referring to a secret plan the leaders had to join with Egypt and combat the Assyrians, which they were trying to hide from the Lord because He had counseled otherwise.

16. HE DID NOT MAKE ME: For humans to make plans on their own without God is a rejection of God as their Creator. Paul later reasoned that it is also a questioning of the sovereignty of God (see Romans 9:19–21). The clay is not equal with the divine potter!

17. FRUITFUL FIELD . . . FOREST: In the future, a reversal of roles between the mighty and the weak will transpire when God intervenes to bless Jerusalem. The moral change in the Jewish nation will be as great as if the usually forested Lebanon were turned into a field and vice versa.

18. BLIND SHALL SEE: The spiritual blindness of Israel will no longer exist.

19–20. INCREASE THEIR JOY . . . CUT OFF: The future messianic age will bring a reversal of status. Rejoicing will replace the hardships of the oppressed. The oppressors' dominance will end.

22. NOT NOW BE ASHAMED: Israel had frequently suffered disgrace, but this would change at the personal presence of the Messiah. After the salvation of Israel in the end time, the children of Jacob will no longer cause their forefathers to blush over their wickedness.

23. FEAR THE GOD OF ISRAEL: Jacob's descendants will marvel at the strong deliverance of the Lord and set Him apart as the only one worthy of utmost respect.

24. COME TO UNDERSTANDING: With their newfound respect for God, the formerly wayward will gain the capacity for spiritual perception.

RESCUE GONE WRONG: Isaiah again points out the futility of Judah trusting in a foreign power for rescue instead of trusting in God.

30:1. NOT OF ME . . . NOT OF MY SPIRIT: Hezekiah's advisers urged him to turn to the Egyptians, not to God, for help against the invading Assyrians.

Isaiah denounces this reliance on Egypt rather than God, who had forbidden such alliances.

2. NOT ASKED MY ADVICE: They had failed to consult God's prophet.

3. SHALL BE YOUR SHAME . . . HUMILIATION: The Assyrians had already defeated the Egyptian army only 100 miles from the Egyptian border.

6. THROUGH A LAND OF TROUBLE AND ANGUISH . . . CAMELS: Isaiah pictures a rich caravan, trudging slowly through rugged territory fraught with dangers, on its way to Egypt to purchase assistance.

7. RAHAB-HEM-SHEBETH: Isaiah calls the powerful Egypt, which was unwilling to help Judah, the name *Rahab*, meaning "strength" or "sitting idle" (Hebrew).

8. FOR TIME TO COME: God instructed Isaiah to make a permanent, written record so future generations could learn Israel's folly of trusting in Egypt instead of in the Lord.

10–11. SPEAK TO US SMOOTH THINGS . . . TURN ASIDE FROM THE PATH: Isaiah's listeners were tired of hearing counsel contrary to the path they desired to follow and wanted him to change his message to accommodate them.

12. THIS WORD: The instruction of the Lord through Isaiah. Since the people had opted not to hear the word of the Lord's prophet, they will now hear from the Lord's judgment.

13–14. HIGH WALL . . . POTTER'S VESSEL: These portray the coming disaster to befall the rebels: (1) a high wall that collapses suddenly, and (2) a clay jug that shatters into pieces when dropped.

16. WE WILL RIDE ON SWIFT HORSES: The people put their trust in Egypt's horses instead of the Lord. But no horse could deliver them from their God-appointed oppressors.

> GOD'S TIMING: *Isaiah prophesies that God will extend His grace to*
> *His people, in His own timing, as His people choose to wait on Him.*

18. THE LORD WILL WAIT: Judah would not wait on the Lord to deliver them, so He would wait to be gracious to the nation.

19. DWELL IN ZION AT JERUSALEM: Isaiah emphatically points to a result of God's grace toward Israel—the survival of the city of Jerusalem as the center of her domain.

20. EYES SHALL SEE: After Israel's period of judgment for disobedience, God will open their eyes to the soundness of the message of His prophets.

21. A WORD BEHIND YOU: The teachers will be near and the pupils sensitive to the Lord's prophets, in strong contrast to the callousness formerly manifest (see Isaiah 29:10–11).

22. THROW THEM AWAY: The Babylonian captivity rid Israel of her idolatry in fulfillment of this prophecy.

23–25. OXEN . . . DONKEYS: In the messianic kingdom of the future day, agriculture, cattle raising, food production, and water resources will prosper. The prophet predicts the redemption of all nature (see Romans 8:19–21).

25. TOWERS FALL: Powerful nations that oppress Israel will come to an end.

26. LIGHT OF THE MOON . . . LIGHT OF THE SUN: The benefits from the natural bodies of light will be much greater. The increase in the intensity of their light will work to people's advantage, not to their detriment (as in Revelation 16:8–9).

JUDGMENT ON ASSYRIA: Isaiah follows the promise of Judah's redemption with a promise of Assyria's destruction.

27. THE NAME OF THE LORD: His name focuses particularly on His revealed character as Sovereign and Savior.

27–28. COMES FROM AFAR . . . OVERFLOWING STREAM: The Lord will come suddenly upon His enemies, like a great storm with its accompanying flood, to overwhelm them.

29. A HOLY FESTIVAL . . . GLADNESS OF HEART: While God's judgment devastates the Assyrians, the people of Jerusalem conduct a time of joyful celebration as at one of their feasts, perhaps a Passover.

31. ASSYRIA WILL BE BEATEN DOWN: This refers to Assyria in particular, but in the long range, any enemy of God's people will fall victim to divine storm and flood.

32. TAMBOURINES AND HARPS: With each blow of punishment against the Assyrians will come joyful celebration in Jerusalem.

33. TOPHET: Literally a place of abomination. Idolatrous Israel had burned human victims in this valley, an area sometimes called the Valley of Hinnom (see 2 Kings 23:10). Later, it became known as Gehenna, the place of refuse for the city, with constantly burning fires, symbolizing hell. The defeat was to be so complete that the fire burns continually.

Read Isaiah 35:1–10, noting the key words and phrases indicated below.

> FUTURE GLORY: *Isaiah reveals the future glory of Zion, showing how during the Messiah's reign on earth, the whole world will become a flourishing garden.*

35:1. THE DESERT SHALL REJOICE: Dramatic changes in the land are to come during the messianic age (see Isaiah 30:23–25; 32:15–20).

2. LEBANON . . . CARMEL AND SHARON: These areas near the sea were noted for their agricultural fertility.

THEY SHALL SEE: Israel is to recognize the earth's newfound fruitfulness as coming from the Lord and will attribute to Him the appropriate credit.

3. WEAK HANDS . . . FEEBLE KNEES: The future change in Israel's international role will encourage the discouraged among the people. The writer of Hebrews gave an additional application of this verse to strengthen endurance among Christians suffering persecution for their faith (see Hebrews 12:12).

4. VENGEANCE . . . HE WILL COME AND SAVE YOU: The vengeance of God will furnish the means to redeem His long-oppressed people of Israel.

5. EYES . . . OPENED . . . EARS . . . UNSTOPPED: This is to reverse the spiritual condition of the immediate objects of Isaiah's ministry.

6. LAME SHALL LEAP . . . THE DUMB SING: God's restoration in the millennial age will include physical restoration to the afflicted. Jesus' First Coming gave a foretaste of that future day (see Matthew 11:5; 12:22; Mark 7:37; Luke 7:21; Acts 3:8).

6–7. STREAMS IN THE DESERT: Water was (and is) a precious commodity in Israel. But in the Millennium, there will be no scarcity.

7. HABITATION OF JACKALS: The rocky crags normally inhabited by jackals are to become splashy meadows.

8. HIGHWAY OF HOLINESS: This refers to the way leading the redeemed back to Jerusalem, the throne of Messiah, literally and spiritually. Christ Himself is to be the leader on that way.

9. NO LION SHALL BE THERE: No ferocious beasts are to threaten the safety of those traveling the Highway of Holiness.

THE REDEEMED: Mentioned only rarely in Isaiah 1–39, where the primary theme is God's judgment. However, terms for redemption occur frequently in Isaiah 40–66.

10. SORROW AND SIGHING SHALL FLEE: Gladness is to replace sadness in the day of Israel's restoration.

UNLEASHING THE TEXT

1) How should we understand the emphasis in Isaiah 28 on drinking wine and intoxication?

_____

_____

_____

_____

_____

_____

2) Looking at Isaiah 30, what were some of the reasons God's people wanted to turn to Egypt for rescue?

_____

_____

_____

_____

_____

_____

3) What does Isaiah say in these prophecies about God's timing? Why is it important for God's people to wait upon Him?

_____

_____

_____

_____

_____

4) In Isaiah 35, the prophet discusses the future glory of Zion. What particular passages and images caught your attention? Why?

_____

_____

_____

_____

_____

_____

EXPLORING THE MEANING

Jesus is our Cornerstone. Most of the prophets included strong imagery and visual language in their prophecies, and Isaiah was no exception. In fact, many of the most famous passages recorded in his book are centered on key images. We find one such image in Isaiah 28:16: "Therefore thus says the Lord GOD: 'Behold, I lay in Zion a stone for a foundation, a tried stone, a precious cornerstone, a sure foundation; whoever believes will not act hastily.'"

The image of a cornerstone would have been clear for the people of Isaiah's day. Buildings in that time were generally constructed on top of a stone foundation—with the cornerstone serving as the first and most important piece. Every other stone in that foundation would be laid to match and support the cornerstone. Therefore, if the cornerstone were faulty or set improperly, the entire building would be suspect.

By using that analogy, Isaiah was creating a contrast between the kings and leaders of his day and the future Messiah. The current kings of Israel and Judah were fickle and unreliable—flawed and faulty cornerstones. In the future, however, God would send His Messiah to serve as a sure and certain foundation for His people and His kingdom.

Jesus revealed that He Himself is the cornerstone (see Mark 12:10), and the New Testament consistently affirms that this imagery pointed to Christ as the foundation of the church. Paul wrote, "Now, therefore, you are no longer strangers and foreigners, but fellow citizens with the saints and members of the household of God, having been built on the foundation of the apostles and prophets, Jesus Christ Himself being the chief cornerstone, in whom the whole building, being fitted together, grows into a holy temple in the Lord" (Ephesians 2:19–21). Peter also referenced Isaiah's cornerstone in his first epistle (see 1 Peter 2:6).

We cannot take matters into our own hands. As we have seen, the leaders of Judah found themselves between a rock and a hard place. Their neighbors, including Israel and Samaria, had been hostile for decades. Now, a more distant enemy, Assyria, had arrived on the scene with a reputation for war and brutal conquest—and with Jerusalem as a target.

Given the many ways that God had intervened to save and strengthen His people in the past, those in the courts of Jerusalem should have immediately turned to Him for rescue. Instead, they came up with a different plan: *Egypt*. Specifically, many believed a military alliance with Egypt would provide the force needed to withstand the Assyrian army. Through Isaiah, God was specific in His rejection of this plan: "'Woe to the rebellious children,' says the LORD . . . 'who walk to go down to Egypt, and have not asked My advice, to strengthen themselves in the strength of Pharaoh, and to trust in the shadow of Egypt!'" (Isaiah 30:1–2).

There are many moments in Scripture that follow a similar pattern of people taking matters into their own hands rather than trusting God's plan. Abraham took matters into his own hands when he fathered Ishmael through Hagar, rather than waiting for God's promised child to be born through Sarah. Jacob took matters into his own hands when he stole the family blessing through deceit, rather than trusting God. Saul took matters into his own hands when he kept the flocks and herds of the Amalekites, rather than destroying them as God had commanded. As a result, he lost God's blessing, and David was anointed to replace him as king.

We set ourselves up for failure when our primary trust is in human means, including our own resourcefulness. The true way of blessing is trust in God's strength and obedience to His plans.

God has laid the path for His people. Rather than taking matters into our own hands, God's people must follow the path He has laid before us. Isaiah described that path as "the Highway of Holiness" (35:8). Speaking of that road, he said, "The unclean shall not pass over it" (verse 8), and, "No lion shall be there, nor shall any ravenous beast go up on it" (verse 9). Instead, "the redeemed shall walk there, and the ransomed of the LORD shall return, and come to Zion with singing, with everlasting joy on their heads. They shall obtain joy and gladness, and sorrow and sighing shall flee away" (verses 9–10).

In speaking of this road, Isaiah was pointing forward to when Christ will reign over all the earth. In that day, "the eyes of the blind shall be opened, and the ears of the deaf shall be unstopped. Then the lame shall leap like a deer, and the tongue of the dumb sing. For waters shall burst forth in the wilderness, and streams in the desert" (verses 5–6).

Jesus referenced Isaiah's image of that road several times in His public teaching. In fact, He revealed that He Himself is the "Highway of Holiness," saying, "I am the way, the truth, and the life. No one comes to the Father except through Me" (John 14:6). Jesus also described the way of this world as a broad road, with a broad gate, that leads to destruction. In contrast, "narrow is the gate and difficult is the way which leads to life, and there are few who find it" (Matthew 7:14). Instead of trusting our own resources, which leads to destruction, we must obey God by following Christ.

REFLECTING ON THE TEXT

5)   What does it mean to the church that Christ is its cornerstone?

_____

_____

_____

_____

6)   What are the benefits of building our lives on Christ rather than our own resources?

_____

_____

_____

_____

7)   When have you taken matters into your own hands during a key moment or decision? What happened as a result?

_____

_____

_____

_____

8) How is God's "Highway of Holiness" different from the "broad way" offered by our world?

_____

_____

_____

_____

_____

PERSONAL RESPONSE

9) What are some factors that often cause you to rely on your own strength rather than trusting in God?

_____

_____

_____

_____

_____

10) Who or what is serving as an "Egypt" in your life today? In other words, who or what are you relying on rather than God?

_____

_____

_____

_____

_____

7

HISTORICAL INTERLUDE
Isaiah 36:1–39:8

DRAWING NEAR
What are some important historical moments that you have experienced during your lifetime?

_____

_____

_____

_____

_____

_____

_____

_____

_____

_____

_____

_____

_____

_____

THE CONTEXT
As a whole, the prophets wrote during moments and circumstances that were critical to the history of God's people. They served as God's mouthpieces, offering instruction, warning, rebuke, and inspiration during such pivotal times in Israel and Judah. While we have some indications of when they served among God's people, the prophets weren't primarily interested in preserving a detailed

historical record. However, the passages from Isaiah that we will explore in this lesson are an exception.

The passages we read in Isaiah 36–39 duplicate (almost verbatim) 2 Kings 18:13–20:19, which is a record of Assyria's attempt to conquer Jerusalem. Isaiah added this material to make the references to Assyria more understandable. For this reason, it is most likely that Isaiah is the author of this section, since 2 Chronicles 32:32 says Isaiah also wrote the acts of Hezekiah. Isaiah's record was then incorporated into 2 Kings by the author of that record.

These chapters in Isaiah form the transition that closes the first division of Isaiah's prophecy. Isaiah 36 and 37 are the historical consummation of Isaiah 1–35, which describe Jerusalem's deliverance from Assyria. Isaiah 38 and 39 are the historical basis for Isaiah 40–66, which offer a preview of Judah's captivity at the hands of the Babylonians.

KEYS TO THE TEXT

Read Isaiah 36:1–39:8, noting the key words and phrases indicated below.

> *A TERRIFYING ATTACK: Isaiah shifts from prophesying about Judah and her enemies to describing Assyria's attack and attempt to conquer Jerusalem.*

36:1. FOURTEENTH YEAR OF KING HEZEKIAH: Sennacherib's attack came in 701 BC, so this places the beginning of Hezekiah's reign at 715 BC. In 2 Kings 18:1, we read that he began to reign in the third year of Hoshea, c. 729 BC, but Hezekiah served as co-regent with Ahaz (c. 729–716 BC) before assuming the throne exclusively. It was customary for the later kings of Israel to bring their sons into partnership in the government during their lives.

SENNACHERIB: The king of Assyria (c. 705 to 681 BC).

FORTIFIED CITIES: The discovery of the ancient *Annals of Sennacherib* reveals the cities he conquered in his campaign southward from Sidon on the Mediterranean coast.

2. RABSHAKEH: The spokesman for Sennacherib's three highest officials, who represented the king against Jerusalem on this occasion (see 2 Kings 18:17).

GREAT ARMY: This was a token force of the main army, with which Sennacherib hoped to bluff Judah into submitting.

LACHISH: A city about twenty-five miles southwest of Jerusalem. Sennacherib's conquest of this city was in its closing phase when he sent the messengers.

AQUEDUCT FROM THE UPPER POOL: Isaiah met Ahaz at the same spot in his unsuccessful attempt to dissuade him from trusting in foreign powers (see Isaiah 7:3).

3. JOAH . . . THE RECORDER: The position was that of an intermediary between the king and the people.

4–10. RABSHAKEH SAID TO THEM: Rabshakeh's logic was twofold: (1) Egypt was unable to deliver Jerusalem, and (2) the Lord had called on the Assyrians to destroy Judah.

4. GREAT KING, THE KING OF ASSYRIA: This is the self-appropriated title of Assyrian kings. In contrast, Rabshakeh omitted any title for Hezekiah.

5. MERE WORDS: Words amounted to nothing when it came to warfare. In other words, Judah was defenseless.

6. BROKEN REED: The Assyrian's advice strongly resembles that of Isaiah (see Isaiah 19:14–16; 30:7; 31:3).

7. HE WHOSE HIGH PLACES AND WHOSE ALTARS: Rabshakeh mistakenly thought Hezekiah's reforms in removing idols (see 2 Kings 18:4) had removed opportunities to worship the Lord.

THIS ALTAR: That all worship should center in Solomon's temple was utterly foreign to the polytheistic Assyrians.

8–9. I URGE YOU: Rabshakeh here taunts and minimizes Judah's best defensive efforts, even with Egypt's help.

10. THE LORD SAID: Rabshakeh's boastful claim of the authority from Judah's God for his mission may have been a ploy on his part to get a surrender, but it aligned with Isaiah's prophecy that the Assyrians would be His instrument to punish His people. The Assyrians may have heard this from partisans, or may not have known this, but Judah did.

11. ARAMAIC . . . HEBREW: Hezekiah's representatives, aware of the alarm created by the suggestion that the Lord was on the Assyrian side, ask Rabshekah to change from Hebrew to Aramaic so that the people on the wall would not understand his words and be terrified.

12. MEN . . . ON THE WALL: The foreign emissary continues his efforts to damage the city's morale by speaking of the horrors of famine that a long siege would involve.

13. CALLED OUT WITH A LOUD VOICE: Rabshakeh speaks longer and louder, suggesting that Hezekiah could not save the city, but that the great king, the king of Assyria, would fill the people with abundance (see verses 16–17).

16. MAKE PEACE WITH ME BY A PRESENT: Literally, "Make a blessing with me." The official is inviting the people to make a covenant with Assyria by surrendering.

17. TAKE YOU AWAY: Rabshakeh does not hide Assyria's well-known practice of deporting conquered peoples to distant places.

18–20. HAS ANY ONE OF THE GODS: In Rabshakeh's eyes, the Lord is just one of the many gods worshiped by nations conquered by the Assyrians.

21. HELD THEIR PEACE: Hezekiah had apparently anticipated the ultimatum of the Assyrians and had told his representatives and the men on the wall not to respond.

22. CLOTHES TORN: The king's representatives return to him in a state of grief and shock at the blasphemy they thought they had heard.

ISAIAH ASSURES HEZEKIAH: King Hezekiah responds to the Assyrian threat with mourning and prayer to the Lord. God responds by sending Isaiah to speak with the king and reassure him that Judah will be delivered.

37:1. TORE HIS CLOTHES . . . SACKCLOTH: A reaction that symbolizes Hezekiah's grief, repentance, and contrition. The nation was to repent, and the king was to lead the way.

HOUSE OF THE LORD: God had designated the temple as His "house of prayer" (see Isaiah 56:7), so it was the proper place to confess sins and seek forgiveness.

2. ELDERS OF THE PRIESTS: These were senior religious leaders in Israel.

3. COME TO BIRTH . . . NO STRENGTH: Hezekiah compares his dilemma to a mother in labor who is unable to deliver her child. Jerusalem had to be delivered, but he was helpless to make it happen.

4. REPROACH THE LIVING GOD: Hezekiah, receiving the report of Rabshakeh's belittling the Lord by equating Him with other gods, responds by pointing out the distinction between *the* God, who is living, and gods who are lifeless and helpless.

REMNANT THAT IS LEFT: Only Jerusalem remained unconquered.

6. DO NOT BE AFRAID: This is the same assurance that Isaiah gave to Ahaz (see Isaiah 7:4).

7. I WILL SEND A SPIRIT: The Lord promises to incline Sennacherib's attitude in such a way that he will leave Jerusalem unharmed and return home.

8. LIBNAH: After conquering Lachish, Sennacherib moves on to this smaller town to the north of Lachish.

9. TIRHAKAH KING OF ETHIOPIA: Tirhakah did not become king of Ethiopia (and Egypt) until eleven years after the 701 BC siege, so Isaiah's use of "king" anticipates his future title. At this moment, however, he represented a threat to Sennacherib from the south that caused him to renew his call for Jerusalem's surrender to the north.

10–13. THUS YOU SHALL SPEAK TO HEZEKIAH KING OF JUDAH: The king of Assyria sent messengers to summarize the arguments given in Rabshakeh's ultimatum (see Isaiah 36:4–19).

10. DECEIVE: The accusation of deception was first made against Hezekiah (see Isaiah 36:14), and then against the Lord.

12. GOZAN AND HARAN AND REZEPH ... TELASSAR: These conquered cities lay between the Tigris and Euphrates rivers in Mesopotamia.

13. HAMATH ... ARPAD ... SEPHARVAIM, HENA, AND IVAH: These cities in Syria had recently fallen to the Assyrians.

14. HOUSE OF THE LORD: Godly Hezekiah returns to the house of the Lord as he should have, in contrast to Ahaz, who in a similar crisis refused even to ask a sign from the Lord.

16. YOU HAVE MADE HEAVEN AND EARTH: The basis for Hezekiah's plea is God's role as the Sovereign and Creator of the universe, not Judah's worthiness to be delivered.

17. HEAR ... AND SEE: In contrast to the gods of other nations, the God of Israel heard and saw everything.

18–19. THEY WERE NOT GODS: Hezekiah here dismantles the Assyrian theory that the Lord was no different from gods of the other nations that could not deliver their worshipers.

20. YOU ALONE: Hezekiah displays the highest motivation of all in requesting the salvation of Jerusalem: that the world may know that the Lord alone is God.

GOD'S WORD CONCERNING SENNACHERIB: *The Lord God responds to King Hezekiah's prayer with His judgment against the Assyrian king.*

21. ISAIAH THE SON OF AMOZ: Isaiah receives a response from the Lord immediately upon the conclusion of Hezekiah's prayer

22. LAUGHED YOU TO SCORN: Jerusalem, portrayed as a helpless virgin before a would-be rapist, would have the last laugh against Sennacherib.

23. YOU REPROACHED AND BLASPHEMED: The Lord heard Sennacherib's reproach against Him.

24–25. BY YOUR SERVANTS: Even the servants of Sennacherib had bragged about Assyria's being unstoppable.

26. I HAVE BROUGHT IT TO PASS: God corrects Sennacherib's vanity. The Assyrian king had conquered nothing on his own but was a mere instrument in the Lord's hand.

27. THEY WERE DISMAYED: Assyria had utterly overwhelmed populations in their conquests.

28. YOUR RAGE AGAINST ME: Sennacherib's ignorance of being a mere tool in the Lord's hand was bad, but his belittling of God, the source of his life, was far worse.

29. HOOK IN YOUR NOSE. . . BRIDLE : In judging Sennacherib, the Lord treats him as an obstinate animal with a ring in his nose and/or a bridle in his mouth. Some ancient sources indicate that captives were led before a king by a cord attached to a hook or ring through the upper lip and nose. Thus was Sennacherib to be brought back to his own country.

30. A SIGN TO YOU: The two years in which Judah was sustained by the growth of their crops were the two in which Sennacherib ravaged them (see Isaiah 32:10). He left immediately after the deliverance, so in the third year the people left could plant again.

31. THE REMNANT: The remnant of survivors in Jerusalem would produce descendants to cover the land once again.

32. ZEAL OF THE LORD OF HOSTS: The same confirmation of God's promise in Isaiah 9:7 assured the future establishment of the messianic kingdom. Deliverance from Sennacherib in Hezekiah's day was a down payment on the literal, final restoration of Israel.

33. SHALL NOT COME: God promises that the Assyrians will not even pose a physical threat to Jerusalem. They came near, but never engaged in a true siege of the city.

34. SHALL HE RETURN: In contrast with Sennacherib's arrival in Judah as an overbearing, invincible monarch, he returned to Assyria as a defeated, dejected "has been." In his own *Annals*, he claimed only to have "shut up" Jerusalem, not to have conquered it.

35. FOR MY OWN SAKE: Sennacherib had directly challenged the Lord's faithfulness to His word, so the faithfulness of God was at stake in this contest with the Assyrians.

FOR MY SERVANT DAVID'S SAKE: God had pledged to perpetuate David's line on his throne (see 2 Samuel 7:16).

36. THE ANGEL OF THE LORD: This is Isaiah's only use of a title that is frequent in the Old Testament, one referring to the Lord Himself.

KILLED IN THE CAMP: Secular records also mention this massive slaughter of Assyrian troops, without noting its supernatural nature.

37. NINEVEH: The capital of Assyria.

38. HIS GOD: The place of Sennacherib's death (c. 681 BC) recalled the impotence of his god, Nisroch, compared with the omnipotence of Hezekiah's God.

STRUCK HIM DOWN: Sennacherib's pitiful death came twenty years after his confrontation with the Lord regarding the fate of Jerusalem.

ARARAT: The mountain region north of Israel, west of Assyria.

ESARHADDON: The successor to Sennacherib (c. 681–669 BC).

A PERSONAL PRAYER: Isaiah relates how earlier in the reign of King Hezekiah of Judah, when he was sick and at the point of death, he turned to God for rescue.

38:1. HEZEKIAH WAS SICK: Hezekiah's sickness occurred before the Assyrian siege of Jerusalem described Isaiah 36–37. Isaiah places the description of that illness here, along with chapter 39, to introduce chapters 40–66.

SET YOUR HOUSE IN ORDER: An instruction telling Hezekiah to make his final will known to his family (see also 2 Samuel 17:23; 1 Kings 2:1–9).

YOU SHALL DIE AND NOT LIVE: The prediction sounded final, but Hezekiah knew God was willing to hear his appeal.

3. LOYAL HEART: Hezekiah bases his implied request for an extension of his life on an undivided desire to please the Lord.

5. I WILL ADD TO YOUR DAYS: The Lord's immediate response was to grant the king's request. Isaiah was not alarmed by having to reverse a prophecy so quickly, as Jonah was later on (see Jonah 4:2–3). Isaiah resembled Nathan in this respect (see 2 Samuel 7:3–6).

6. I WILL DELIVER . . . THIS CITY: The deliverance described in the previous chapter.

8. TEN DEGREES BACKWARD: This is the first biblical mention of any means of marking time. Hezekiah requested this sign to confirm the Lord's promise of healing (see 2 Kings 20:8–10).

9. WRITING OF HEZEKIAH: In response to his healing, Hezekiah wrote the record of his helplessness when facing death (see verses 10–14) and told of God's response to His condition (see verses 15–20). This poetry is missing from the parallel account in 2 Kings.

10. IN THE PRIME OF MY LIFE: The king was probably in his thirties or forties when he fell sick.

11. I SHALL NOT SEE: Hezekiah feared that death would terminate his fellowship with God.

YAH: The Hebrew repeats the name: "YAH, YAH." In the King James Version, this is rendered, "LORD, even the LORD."

12. SHEPHERD'S TENT . . . A WEAVER: These two comparisons with transient articles illustrate how death removes, in a moment, what may have seemed so permanent.

14. I MOURNED . . . UNDERTAKE FOR ME!: In his helplessness, Hezekiah pleaded with God to deliver him from impending death.

15. HE HIMSELF HAS DONE IT: The king had complete confidence in God.

16. RESTORE ME AND MAKE ME LIVE: The king's survival was God's accomplishment.

17. SINS BEHIND YOUR BACK: Hezekiah felt his sickness was somehow related to his sinfulness. To be rid of the latter was also to be rid of the former.

18. CANNOT HOPE: Hezekiah's understanding of the resurrection of believers was incomplete. But he was right in recognizing that death ended his opportunity for earthly praise and worship in the presence of men.

19. THE FATHER . . . TO THE CHILDREN: Word about God's faithfulness was passed from generation to generation. If Hezekiah had no heir at this point, he had another reason for frustration over dying in the prime of life.

20. THEREFORE WE WILL SING: Hezekiah was so overwhelmed with gratitude to God that he felt compelled to express it appropriately throughout the fifteen years he had left on earth.

21–22. POULTICE ON THE BOIL: These final two verses furnish background details of the account given in verses 1–8. "Poultice" refers to the medicine for healing the king's sickness.

22. WHAT IS THE SIGN: Hezekiah's request explains why the Lord gave him a sign that he would be healed (see verse 7).

THE HOUSE OF THE LORD: Hezekiah went to the temple as Isaiah had instructed him to do.

A FUTURE THREAT: Although God had promised that Assyria would not conquer Jerusalem, this chapter gives a foreshadowing of the moment when Babylon eventually destroyed that city as God's instrument of judgment.

39:1. AT THAT TIME: This occurs just after Hezekiah's sickness and recovery.

2. HEZEKIAH WAS PLEASED: Isaiah does not say whether Hezekiah was pleased because of flattery or because of a desire for help against the increasing Assyrian threat.

HIS TREASURES: Hezekiah, doubtless in an attempt to try and impress his visitors, shows them all he can contribute in an alliance against the Assyrians.

3. ISAIAH THE PROPHET WENT: God's spokesman shows up, uninvited, to confront the king, as often happened (see, for example, 2 Samuel 12:1; 1 Kings 13:1; 18:16–17).

5–6. WORD OF THE LORD: Isaiah predicts the Babylonian captivity that would come more than a century later (in 586 BC), another prophecy historically fulfilled in all of its expected detail.

6. NOTHING SHALL BE LEFT: Hezekiah's sin of parading his wealth before the visitors backfires, though this sin was only symptomatic of the ultimate reason for the captivity. The major cause was the corrupt leadership of Manasseh, Hezekiah's son (see 2 Kings 21:11–15).

7. SONS WHO WILL DESCEND FROM YOU: To a king without an heir, this was good news (that he would have one someday) and bad news (that some of his sons must go into captivity).

8. WORD OF THE LORD . . . GOOD: This is a surprising response from Hezekiah to the negative prophecy that Isaiah just delivered! It perhaps acknowledged Isaiah as God's faithful messenger.

PEACE AND TRUTH IN MY DAYS: Hezekiah might have reacted selfishly, or possibly he looked for a bright spot to lighten the gloomy fate of his descendants.

UNLEASHING THE TEXT

1) How did Assyria's representative attempt to undermine the people's confidence in both God and their king in his speeches in Isaiah 36? Explain.

_____

_____

_____

_____

_____

2) What are your impressions of King Hezekiah from reading this section?

_____

_____

_____

_____

_____

3) When has God answered your prayers in a definitive way?

_____

_____

_____

_____

_____

4) How would you summarize Hezekiah's mistake related in Isaiah 39?

_____

_____

_____

_____

_____

_____

EXPLORING THE MEANING

Temptation strikes at our trust in God. The people of Judah, with a portion of the Assyrian army arrayed against them, gathered together in the fortified city of Jerusalem for safety. An Assyrian representative came to speak with the residents of Jerusalem, encouraging them to surrender willingly rather than risk a prolonged siege and eventual slaughter. This representative in the book of Isaiah is called "the Rabshakeh." His message can be boiled down to a single idea: *God cannot save you.*

During Satan's temptation of Adam and Eve in the Garden of Eden, the devil sought to drive a wedge between God and humanity by questioning the Lord's goodness and reliability (see Genesis 3). Satan also used positive elements to complement his temptation, showing Adam and Eve that the forbidden fruit "was good for food, that it was pleasant to the eyes, and a tree desirable to make one wise" (verse 6).

In a similar way, the Rabshakeh tried to entice the people of Jerusalem with food and comfort. "Do not listen to Hezekiah; for thus says the king of Assyria: 'Make peace with me by a present and come out to me; and every one of you eat from his own vine and every one from his own fig tree, and every one of you drink the waters of his own cistern; until I come and take you away to a land like your own land, a land of grain and new wine, a land of bread and vineyards" (Isaiah 36:16–17). Later, he struck at the people's trust in God, asking, "Who among all the gods of these lands have delivered their countries from my hand, that the LORD should deliver Jerusalem from my hand?" (verse 20).

These same patterns exist today. Satan seeks to separate us from God by suggesting that He cannot be trusted and by pointing at temporary pleasures as an alternative to obeying God's will. Don't be fooled! Rather, stand strong and trust in God's goodness and sovereignty.

God is always faithful to His people, and more powerful than their circumstances. The people of Judah were under a real and present danger because of Assyria's army. They were in trouble, and they knew it. So God spoke through Isaiah, promising all would be well if the people trusted in Him: "Thus says the LORD: 'Do not be afraid of the words which you have heard, with which the servants of the king of Assyria have blasphemed Me. Surely I will send a spirit upon him, and he shall hear a rumor and return to his own land; and I will cause him to fall by the sword in his own land'" (37:6–7).

King Hezekiah and the people of Judah listened to God. They trusted Him. They obeyed. And God was faithful to His promise. When the Rabshakeh returned to his own people, he "found the king of Assyria warring against Libnah, for he heard that he had departed from Lachish. And the king heard concerning Tirhakah king of Ethiopia, 'He has come out to make war with you'" (verses 8–9). Essentially, the Assyrians became threatened by other enemies and withdrew from Jerusalem—never to return.

Later, God's promise was ultimately fulfilled when Sennacherib, king of Assyria, was murdered by his own sons while worshiping a false god (see verse 38). God proved His faithfulness to the people of Israel and Judah again and again—yet His faithfulness is not limited to antiquity. He is still faithful today!

The best prayers are honest prayers. Hezekiah was the king of Judah during this time of attack from Assyria, and he is notable among Judah's kings as someone who understood the value of prayer. When Sennacherib had to withdraw from Jerusalem to deal with other attackers, he sent a letter to Hezekiah promising to return and finish his intended conquest. That turned out to be an empty threat, but no one knew it at the time.

For that reason, it's important to note what Hezekiah did in response. First, he went up to the temple and spread out the letter before God. Then he prayed: "O LORD of hosts, God of Israel, the One who dwells between the cherubim, You are God, You alone, of all the kingdoms of the earth. You have made heaven and earth. Incline Your ear, O Lord, and hear; open Your eyes, O Lord, and see; and hear all the words of Sennacherib, which he has sent to reproach the living God" (Isaiah 37:16–17). Hezekiah asked God to save the people of Judah so "all the kingdoms of the earth may know that You are the LORD, You alone" (verse 20).

At another time during his reign, Hezekiah had experienced a profound sickness. God told Isaiah to give Hezekiah the news that that sickness would be fatal. Here is how the king responded: "Hezekiah turned his face toward the wall, and prayed to the LORD, and said, 'Remember now, O LORD, I pray, how I have walked before You in truth and with a loyal heart, and have done what is good in Your sight.' And Hezekiah wept bitterly" (38:2–3).

In both instances, Hezekiah's prayers were an honest reflection of his troubled heart. He was bitterly disappointed at the thought of his coming death, so he expressed those emotions honestly before God, even to the point of weeping. (Interestingly, God responded to Hezekiah's prayer by granting him fifteen more years of life.) He knew he could not defeat Sennacherib and the armies of Assyria, so he asked God to save his people. The point is this: Our best prayers are those moments when we take God as His Word and speak with Him honestly from our hearts.

REFLECTING ON THE TEXT

5) What are some ways that Satan tries to attack our trust in God today?

_____

_____

_____

_____

6) Why do you trust God? What are your main reasons for trusting Him?

_____

_____

_____

_____

7) How have you seen God display His strength and sovereignty in your circumstances?

_____

_____

_____

_____

_____

8) Describe your current prayer life. What would you like to change?

_____

_____

_____

_____

_____

PERSONAL RESPONSE

9) What steps can you take right now to help you resist temptation in the days to come?

_____

_____

_____

_____

_____

10) Do you have an honest, open line of communication with God? What currently inhibits your prayer life?

_____

_____

_____

_____

_____

8

DELIVERANCE FROM CAPTIVITY
Isaiah 40:1–31; 42:1–25; 44:1–28

DRAWING NEAR
What brings you comfort when you're feeling low or when you are in a difficult situation?

_____

_____

_____

_____

_____

_____

_____

_____

_____

_____

THE CONTEXT
Although Isaiah's prophesies in the first half of his book addressed many different nations and peoples, he was speaking primarily to the residents of Judah, the southern kingdom of God's people. This was his primary audience. As such, the prophecies of Isaiah 1–39 address Judah in her situation during Isaiah's ministry, which stretched from 739 BC until c. 686 BC.

However, a major shift takes place in the second half of Isaiah's book. Specifically, the prophecies of chapters 40–66 address Judah as though the prophesied Babylonian captivity (foretold in Isaiah 39:5–7) were already a present reality—even though that captivity did not begin until 605–586 BC. So, through Isaiah, God was speaking to the people of Judah who would experience captivity a hundred years and more after Isaiah's ministry concluded.

In this lesson, we will also see a shift in the tone of Isaiah's prophecy. Rather than primarily speaking words of judgment, he includes promises and blessing from God to the people of Judah. These promises would have been deeply encouraging to the people of Isaiah's day, but they were also encouraging to those future residents of Judah and Jerusalem who would endure the terror of Babylon's conquest.

KEYS TO THE TEXT

Read Isaiah 40:1–31, noting the key words and phrases indicated below.

> *WORDS OF COMFORT: Through Isaiah, God offers comfort to the future residents of Judah who would endure the destruction of Jerusalem and captivity in Babylon.*

40:1. COMFORT, YES, COMFORT: The prophecy addresses God's prophets, instructing them to emphasize the theme of comfort to a captive people in a foreign land many miles from their home city of Jerusalem. God has good plans for great blessing to Israel in the future because they are His covenant people, who are never to be permanently cast away.

2. INIQUITY IS PARDONED: Cruel slaughter and captivity at the hands of the Babylonians were sufficient payment for the people's past sins. Someday, after their worldwide dispersion, Israel will return to her land in peace and in the glory of Messiah's kingdom.

3–5. THE VOICE OF ONE CRYING THE WILDERNESS: A prophetic exhortation telling Israel to prepare for the revelation of the Lord's glory at the arrival of Messiah. Scripture sees John the Baptist in this role (see Matthew 3:3; Mark 1:3; Luke 3:4–6; John 1:23).

3–4. PREPARE THE WAY: The remnant of Israel could remove obstacles from the coming Messiah's path through repentance from their sins. John the Baptist reminded his listeners of this necessity (see Matthew 3:2), as did Jesus (see Matthew 4:17; Mark 1:15). This practice reflects the custom of some eastern monarchs to send heralds before them to clear away obstacles, make causeways, straighten crooked roads, and level hills.

5. GLORY OF THE LORD: Jerusalem's misery is to end and the Lord's glory is to replace it. Comfort will come to the city, and every person will see God's glorious salvation in the Messiah's future kingdom.

6. ALL FLESH IS GRASS: Isaiah elaborates on how transitory humanity is—here today, gone tomorrow. People pass away like plants under the hot breath of the withering east wind.

8. THE WORD OF OUR GOD STANDS FOREVER: The permanence of God's word guarantees against any deviation from the divine plan. He has promised Jerusalem's deliverance through His coming, so it must happen in that way.

9. YOU WHO BRING GOOD TIDINGS: Like a messenger on a mountain, to be seen and heard by all, the prophet Isaiah calls on the city to proclaim loudly to the rest of Judah's cities the good news of God's presence there.

BEHOLD YOUR GOD!: The restoration of Israel to the land is to include the resumption of God's presence in Jerusalem after many centuries of absence.

10. WITH A STRONG HAND: At Jesus' Second Coming, He will return with power to defeat His enemies and gather the dispersed of Israel to their land.

11. HIS ARM: A picture of God's omnipotence. The same arm that powerfully scatters the Jews all over the earth in judgment is to overcome Israel's oppressors and tenderly feed and lead His flock.

12–14. WHO HAS: Through a series of questions, to which the implied answer is "no one," the prophet emphasizes the omnipotence and omniscience of God—the God whose coming is to bring comfort to Israel.

12. MEASURED THE WATERS . . . IN A BALANCE: God alone has the power to create the physical universe and the earth in perfect balance, weighing mountains and seas perfectly, so that the earth moves perfectly in space.

13. DIRECTED THE SPIRIT: Isaiah points to the incomparable wisdom of God. Paul later alluded to this verse in connection with God's wisdom in dealing with Jews and Gentiles (see Romans 11:34) and God's impartation of wisdom to the believer (1 Corinthians 2:16).

15–17. THE NATIONS ARE AS A DROP: The surrounding nations that had oppressed Israel were insignificant in comparison to the Lord's greatness and power, so they could not prevent His purposes from being accomplished. His deliverance of Israel was certain.

16. BURNT OFFERING: God is so great and worthy of so much worship, that even the large wood and animal resources of Lebanon were insufficient for appropriate offerings to Him.

18–20. MOLDS AN IMAGE: The prophet sarcastically indicates the futility of trying to portray the immensity of God—His power, wisdom, and resources—in the form of a man-made idol.

21. HAVE YOU NOT UNDERSTOOD: Throughout human history, people had heard by special revelation from God that the Lord, not idols, created all things. They had also understood it from natural revelation as human reason looks at creation (see Romans 1:20).

22. SITS ABOVE THE CIRCLE OF THE EARTH: The word "circle" is applicable to the spherical form of the earth, above which God sits. This implies that He upholds and maintains His creation on a continuing basis. As He looks down, people seem like insects to the One who has stretched and spread out the universal heavens.

23. PRINCES . . . JUDGES: God disposes of human leaders according to His will.

25. LIKEN ME . . . EQUAL: Israel was foolish to compare such a sovereign, almighty Lord with the gods of their Babylonian captors.

26. CREATED THESE THINGS: Rather than worshiping the stars, Israel should have seen in them the evidence of God's creatorship. As innumerable as the stars are, He knows every one and named each. Not one of the stars runs astray, but all are held by the forces with which He has endowed the universe to keep them in their orbit and place.

27–31. O JACOB . . . O ISRAEL: The prophet applies the comforting truths he has just related about God (verses 1–26) to Israel's situation in Babylon during the coming captivity.

27. WHY DO YOU SAY: In light of who God is, how could His people in exile have thought He had forgotten them or was ignorant of their condition?

28. NEITHER FAINTS NOR IS WEARY: God was not too weak to act on their behalf, nor was fatigue an obstacle for the Creator in caring for His people. Although even the young and strong become tired and fall, the Ancient of Days never does.

UNSEARCHABLE: To the human mind, God's wisdom is not fully comprehensible in how He chooses to fulfill His promises, as that of delivering Israel.

31. WAIT ON THE LORD: There is a general principle here that patient, praying believers are blessed by the Lord with strength in their trials (see also 2 Corinthians 12:8–10). The Lord also expected His people to be patient and await His coming in glory at the end to fulfill the promises of national deliverance, when believing Israel would become stronger than they had ever been.

Read Isaiah 42:1–25, noting the key words and phrases indicated below.

> THE FIRST SONG: *Isaiah's prophecy now focuses on a future*
> *King who would bless all of Israel. Scripture reveals that this*
> *is Jesus, the Messiah.*

42:1. MY SERVANT: Others deserve the title "my servant," but this personal Servant of the Lord is the Messiah, who was chosen because the Lord delights in Him (see Matthew 3:16–17) and puts His Spirit upon Him (see Isaiah 11:2). This section (verses 1–9) represents the first of four "Servant Songs" referring to the Messiah (see also Isaiah 49:1–13; 50:4–11; 52:13–53:12), which tell of the Servant's gentle manner and worldwide mission.

JUSTICE TO THE GENTILES: At Jesus' Second Coming, He will rule over a kingdom in which justice prevails throughout the world. All the nations of the world will experience the righteousness and justice of the Messiah King.

2. HE WILL NOT CRY OUT: The quiet and submissive demeanor of Christ at His First Advent fulfilled this prophecy (see Matthew 11:28–30; 1 Peter 2:23).

3. BRUISED REED . . . SMOKING FLAX: The Servant will bring comfort and encouragement to the weak and oppressed.

4. JUSTICE IN THE EARTH: Isaiah here looks beyond the First Coming of Christ to His Second Coming. At His Second Coming, He will rule the earth in perfect justice with "a rod of iron" (see Psalm 2:8–9; Revelation 2:27).

5. THUS SAYS GOD THE LORD: God here speaks directly to the Messiah, identified as "You" in verse 6. God's role as Creator of the universe is the basis of certainty for the fulfilling of His will by His Servant, the Messiah.

6. I, THE LORD: God's personal name is the one He explained to Moses as specially symbolic of the unique relationship He bore to Israel (see Exodus 3:14, 15; 6:3). Here, that covenant name guarantees His ministry through the Messiah-Servant.

COVENANT TO THE PEOPLE: The Servant is a covenant in that He personifies and provides the blessings of salvation to God's people Israel. He is the Mediator of a better covenant than the one with Moses—the New Covenant (see Hebrews 8:6, 10–12).

LIGHT TO THE GENTILES: Simeon saw the beginning of this fulfillment at Christ's First Coming (see Luke 2:32). Jesus came as the Messiah of Israel, yet also the Savior of the world. He commanded His followers to preach the gospel to *everyone* (see Matthew 28:19–20). The church, made up mostly of Gentiles grafted into the trunk of blessing, (see Romans 9:24–30; 11:11–24), fulfills this promise, as does the future kingdom on earth, when the Servant will use Israel to enlighten all the nations of the earth.

7. OPEN BLIND EYES . . . BRING OUT PRISONERS: Jesus fulfilled these words when He applied them to miracles of physical healing and freedom from spiritual bondage (see Matthew 11:5; 4:13–16 Luke 4:18). Under the Servant's millennial reign on earth, spiritual perception will replace Israel's spiritual blindness, and her captives will receive freedom.

9. FORMER THINGS . . . NEW THINGS: The "former things" are already fulfilled or about-to-be-fulfilled prophecies of Isaiah. The "new things" pertain to the future accomplishments of the Lord through His Messiah-Servant when He comes.

10. NEW SONG . . . HIS PRAISE: This new song, called for by new manifestations of God's grace, will match the newness of conditions created by the Servant's work of redemption in the kingdom, for which earth's inhabitants will also sing His praise (see Revelation 4:11; 5:9).

13. MIGHTY MAN: As a mighty warrior, the Lord will work through His Servant to overcome all enemies.

14. HELD MY PEACE: God remained silent until the time was ripe to intervene in human affairs. He was not been indifferent to wickedness in the world, but would send His Servant in "the fullness of the time" (Galatians 4:4).

15. I WILL LAY WASTE: God's judgment through His Servant will wreak devastation on the earth (see Revelation 6–19). The reverse of this judgment will be His blessing through the same Messiah subsequently in the millennial kingdom.

16. I WILL LEAD: God's sovereignty will be evident to all as He guides the blind over previously uncharted courses. The spiritually blind will see the way.

18. HEAR, YOU DEAF: The Lord here charges Israel, His servant, with unfaithfulness. In an important contrast, positive qualitives of the Servant (see Isaiah 42:1–7) are personified into an individual, the Messiah, but terms of reproach toward God's servant (as in 42:18, 19, 22–24) are personified in the nation, Israel. Israel, God's "servant" and "messenger," was perfectly fitted with the truth. However, Isaiah's commission to prophesy highlighted the spiritual deafness and blindness of Israel. The people were deaf to the voice of God and blind to spiritual reality and duty.

21. HIS RIGHTEOUSNESS' SAKE: In spite of Israel's deafness, blindness, and defective righteousness, God will uphold His principles of righteousness.

22. A PEOPLE ROBBED AND PLUNDERED . . . PRISON: Exiled and dispersed, Israel was like a caravan in the desert, attacked unmercifully by bandits and imprisoned in caves or dungeons, so that no human deliverer could restore them.

24. WAS IT NOT THE LORD: Judah went into Babylonian exile and worldwide dispersion as punishment by God for their rebellion against Him.

25. THE FURY OF HIS ANGER: The fall of Jerusalem to Babylon in 586 BC did not result from the strength of Babylon. Rather, Israel had to taste the wrath of God because they paid no attention to His ways.

SET HIM ON FIRE: Nebuchadnezzar burned Jerusalem when he conquered it (see 2 Kings 25:8–9).

Read Isaiah 44:1–28, noting the key words and phrases indicated below.

> GOD'S BLESSING: *Under the shadow of more punishment to come,*
> *the prophet speaks of the abundant blessing to be Israel's portion*
> *during the Millennium.*

44:1. ISRAEL WHOM I HAVE CHOSEN: God had chosen His servant, Israel, to be His own eternally, and they need not fear abandonment.

2. JESHURUN: An honored name for Israel, whose root meaning is "right" or "straight." Contrast the root of Jacob, which means "overreacher" or "deceiver."

3. I WILL POUR WATER ON HIM . . . FLOODS: The extensive blessing of physical conditions will favor the nation in the coming kingdom age.

Isaiah's words here are also symbolic of spiritual refreshment to come from the Holy Spirit and God Himself (see Joel 2:28–29).

5. I AM THE LORD'S: In the future golden age of Israel, belonging to the Lord and belonging to God's chosen people will be synonymous. It will be a badge of honor worn without fear.

6. KING OF ISRAEL . . . REDEEMER . . . LORD OF HOSTS: The Lord identified Himself as Israel's King, Redeemer, champion in battle (see Isaiah 1:9), and eternal One (see 41:4).

THE FIRST AND . . . THE LAST: Jesus, in direct affirmation of His deity, called Himself the First and the Last (see Revelation 1:17; 2:8; 22:13).

> A CHALLENGE: *God's exclusive claim to deity prepares the way for another challenge to false gods in this next section of Isaiah's prophecy.*

7. LET HIM DECLARE: If idols can foretell "the things that are coming and shall come," let them predict accurately, as the Lord has done. Since the Jews have had predictions of the future ever since God chose them as His people, they are qualified to be His witnesses.

9–11. ASHAMED . . . ASHAMED . . . ASHAMED: The workmen who manufactured idols were mere men and could make nothing as good as or greater than man. They and others who put their trust in idols had ample reason to fear and be ashamed of such folly.

12–19: THE BLACKSMITH WITH THE TONGS WORKS ONE IN THE COALS: Human workers expended all their energy to produce a beautiful idol, but the best they could make was the likeness of a man, and it could not renew their strength. Yet those who wait on the Lord will renew their strength (see Isaiah 40:28–31).

15. IT SHALL BE FOR A MAN TO BURN: The same humanly nurtured trees, used as fuel for fires to furnish warmth and to cook, also provides wood for people to make idols, which they worship and to which they entrust their prayers and themselves. Nothing could be more foolish than worshiping a piece of wood, while burning the same wood in a fire to keep warm.

20. DECEIVED HEART . . . LIE: Like eating ashes, which provide no nourishment, idolatry is a deception, from which the sinner gets nothing but judgment.

22. BLOTTED OUT . . . YOUR TRANSGRESSIONS: Isaiah here provides further reassurances of God's sovereign grace on behalf of Israel. God has blotted out their sins written in His book against them (see Revelation 20:12). Just as a person can't see what is ahead because it is blocked by a "thick cloud," so God obliterated the sins of those He redeemed.

RETURN TO ME: God has already provided for redemption, even before the cross, but based on it alone. For those who turn from sin and return to Him, there is redemption (because the purchase price for the sinner was paid by the sacrifice of Christ). The Lord calls on His people to repent so they may receive the promised redemption.

23. SING, O HEAVENS: The national redemption of Israel at Christ's Second Coming also includes the redemption of all nature, so the prophet calls on the whole creation to rejoice.

25. BABBLERS . . . DIVINERS: False prophets must suffer the consequences of their deceptive counsel (see Deuteronomy 13:1–5; Joshua 13:22; Jeremiah 27:9; 29:8; 50:36).

26. THE WORD OF HIS SERVANT: The Lord confirms the word of His true prophets, such as of Isaiah. Most specially, God confirmed the word of the Messiah, who is the consummate embodiment of all the prophets and messengers of God.

RAISE UP HER WASTE PLACES: The fall of Jerusalem came in 586 BC when the Babylonians invaded the land. God promised to restore the land to prosperity, the foretaste of restoration coming after seventy years with the help of the Persians (see Isaiah 41:2), but the greater restoration to come in Messiah's kingdom.

28. WHO SAYS OF CYRUS . . . MY SHEPHERD: This prophecy, given a century and a half before Cyrus lived and became king of Persia, predicted God's use of the Persian king to gather the faithful remnant of Israel back to the land. In this role, Cyrus prefigured the Lord's Servant, who will shepherd the sheep of Israel in their final regathering (see Micah 5:4). The title "shepherd" applied to kings as leaders of God's people (see 2 Samuel 5:2; Jeremiah 3:15).

YOU SHALL BE BUILT: In 538 BC, Cyrus decreed the rebuilding of the temple, thus fulfilling Isaiah's prophecy. The returning Jews completed the work in 516 BC (see Ezra 1:1–2; 6:3, 15).

UNLEASHING THE TEXT

1) What are some specific promises of comfort and blessing mentioned throughout these chapters that caught your attention?

_____

_____

_____

_____

2) Isaiah 42 contains a prophecy about the Messiah. How do the first nine verses point to Jesus?

_____

_____

_____

_____

3) How does Isaiah characterize idols and idolatry in this section?

_____

_____

_____

_____

4) What are some similarities and differences between God's use of Cyrus, a foreign king, and the Messiah to accomplish His will?

_____

_____

_____

_____

EXPLORING THE MEANING

God is a God of comfort. As we have noted several times, justice and wrath are key attributes of God's character. Of course, this is a good thing, for otherwise there would be no consequences for evil in our world. Yet it is important to see that God is not exclusively focused on judgment. Indeed, He is also filled with compassion and the desire to comfort those in need.

In Isaiah 40, the focus of the prophecy shifts to a moment 100 years in the future, during which the city of Jerusalem would be destroyed and God's people taken into Babylon as captives. What did God want to communicate to those who would experience such terrors?

"Comfort, yes, comfort My people!"
Says your God.
"Speak comfort to Jerusalem, and cry out to her,
That her warfare is ended,
That her iniquity is pardoned;
For she has received from the LORD's hand
Double for all her sins" (verses 1–2).

Indeed, comfort and blessing are primary themes in the remainder of Isaiah's recorded prophecy—including the promise of a Messiah who would ultimately come to conquer evil and redeem His people.

Isaiah prophesied often about Jesus. Speaking of the Messiah, it is important to note that Isaiah prophesied a great deal about the birth, life, ministry, death, and resurrection of Jesus Christ—and he did so 700 years before the Incarnation. "Behold! My Servant whom I uphold," God declared. "My Elect One in whom My soul delights! I have put My Spirit upon Him; He will bring forth justice to the Gentiles" (Isaiah 42:1).

One of the more interesting aspects of Isaiah's prophesies about the Messiah involves the Gentiles. He repeatedly mentions that Jesus' impact would not be limited to God's chosen people, the Jews, but would spread through all nations. "I will keep You and give You as a covenant to the people, as a light to the Gentiles, to open blind eyes, to bring out prisoners from the prison, those who sit in darkness from the prison house" (verses 6–7).

Isaiah also set up a juxtaposition between the Messiah and other kings—specifically Cyrus, king of the Medo-Persian empire. Decades before the events occurred, God revealed how He would use Cyrus not only to punish the Babylonians for their sin but also to rebuild the city of Jerusalem and God's temple (see Isaiah 45). While earthly kings such as Cyrus were instruments in God's hand, the

Messiah would come as a fully righteous King, ready and able to accomplish God's will for the world.

Idolatry is foolishness. Idolatry was one of the key reasons God's people in Israel and Judah had wandered away from their special relationship to Him. There are many reasons why the Israelites were enticed by the false gods of the surrounding nations. For one thing, many cults used temple prostitutes as part of their "worship" experiences. For another, worshiping idols gave people a sense of comfort and control. It was much more convenient to fashion an idol and make sacrifices in your home, rather than submit yourself to the Creator of the universe.

Isaiah addressed the topic of idolatry from several different angles. In one humorous passage, he describes the foolishness of people's burning one end of a log to provide warmth and to cook their food, and then fashioning the other end into an idol to be worshiped: "And the rest of it he makes into a god, his carved image. He falls down before it and worships it, prays to it and says, 'Deliver me, for you are my god!'" (44:17). Isaiah also declared, "Those who make an image, all of them are useless, and their precious things shall not profit; they are their own witnesses; they neither see nor know, that they may be ashamed" (verse 9).

These references to idols seem archaic, but the truth is that idolatry is not a thing of the past. Rather, idolatry is fully practiced in the modern world—including by those who call themselves Christians. An idol is anything we allow to occupy God's rightful place in our lives. It's anything we worship other than God. Money qualifies as an idol for many people in our culture. So does power, pleasure, entertainment, and comfort. We no longer create carven images in most of the modern world. Yet we often still seek to replace God with items or goals that have no capacity to save, bless, or provide what we truly need.

REFLECTING ON THE TEXT

5) What temporal, short-term solutions do people look to for comfort? How does God's comfort differ?

_____

_____

_____

_____

_____

6) What are some of the ways God's people receive comfort and care from Him?

_____

_____

_____

_____

_____

_____

7) What comfort and assurance did God's people draw from Isaiah's prophecies regarding Messiah? On this side of the cross, how do believers draw similar comfort from Isaiah's words?

_____

_____

_____

_____

_____

_____

8) Where do you see idolatry at work in the world today? In your community?

_____

_____

_____

_____

_____

_____

PERSONAL RESPONSE

9) How can you actively turn to God and seek out His presence when you need comfort?

_____

_____

_____

_____

_____

10) What are some steps that you can take this week to identify any possible idols in your life?

_____

_____

_____

_____

_____

_____

9

THE SERVANT'S MISSION

Isaiah 49:1–50:11; 52:1–53:12

DRAWING NEAR

What role has God called you to in the work of His kingdom?

_____

_____

_____

_____

_____

_____

_____

_____

_____

THE CONTEXT

In the previous lesson, we reviewed the first of four Servant Songs in the book of Isaiah, which are prophetic glimpses forward to the life and ministry of the Messiah. The first of these songs is recorded in Isaiah 42:1–9, and it reveals the Messiah as God's servant in whom His soul delights and on whom His Spirit rests. It also points forward to the Messiah's work, including opening the eyes of the blind and freeing prisoners from their darkness.

In this lesson, we will explore the final three Servant Songs, which include Isaiah 49:1–13, 50:4–11, and 52:13–52:12. In these Scriptures, we will find some of the most poignant and powerful prophesies in the Old Testament about the life and ministry of Jesus. We will explore themes including the restoration of Israel, trusting God, and even the crucifixion of Christ.

KEYS TO THE TEXT

Read Isaiah 49:1–50:11, noting the key words and phrases indicated below.

> THE SECOND SONG: *This second of four Servant Songs tells of the Servant's mission to this world and His spiritual success.*

49:1. FROM THE WOMB; FROM THE MATRIX OF MY MOTHER: The whole world, including the Gentiles (the "people from afar") are called to recognize two points: (1) the Messiah/Servant will be a human being, born as others are of a woman, yet virgin born; and (2) He will be an individual as distinct from a personified group such as the nation of Israel, which has also been called the Lord's servant.

2. MOUTH LIKE A SHARP SWORD: The Lord has given power to His Servant to speak effectively and thereby conquer His enemies. His Word is always effective (see Hebrews 4:12).

HIDDEN ME: The Messiah, before His appearing, was hidden with God, ready to be drawn out at the precise moment.

3. MY SERVANT, O ISRAEL: The Lord's use of the name "Israel" refers here to the Messiah, explainable through the intimate relationship that exists between the nation and her King.

4. LABORED IN VAIN: At His First Coming, the Servant met with rejection by His nation. It may have appeared to some that His mission was a failure because of the suffering and rejection He endured (see John 1:9–11). Although rejected by men, the Servant expresses His strong assurance that He is doing God's work and will be rewarded with complete success.

5. GATHERED TO HIM: The Servant's mission will include the priority of bringing Israel back to the Lord. He will complete this at His Second Advent.

6. RAISE UP THE TRIBES OF JACOB . . . MY SALVATION TO THE ENDS OF THE EARTH: The Servant's goal is the salvation and restoration of Israel for the fulfillment of the covenant promise. But this is not limited to Israel, for He is also to function as a light that brings salvation to the Gentiles. Israel's mission had always been to bring the nations to God. This she will finally do very

effectively during the Tribulation after the conversion of the 144,000 witnesses and when she is restored to her land at the Servant's return to earth (see Revelation 7:1–10; 14:1–5).

7. WHOM MAN DESPISES: This speaks to the humiliating treatment of the Servant at His First Advent, a theme especially emphasized by Isaiah.

WHOM THE NATION ABHORS: The term "nation" is used collectively for all who reject Him, particularly the Gentiles, who are the rulers, kings, and princes referred to as someday giving exalted treatment to the Servant at His Second Advent. Former oppressors will bow down to Him because of the salvation of Israel.

8. ACCEPTABLE TIME: The Messiah is represented as asking for the grace of God to be given to sinners. God gives His favorable answer in a time of grace, when salvation's day comes to the world. At His appointed time in the future, the Lord will, by His Servant, accomplish the final deliverance of Israel. Paul later applied these words to his ministry of proclaiming the gospel of God's grace to all people (see 2 Corinthians 6:2).

A COVENANT TO THE PEOPLE: When the Lord saves and regathers Israel, they will return to the land where Joshua brought their ancestors after their exit from Egypt. It will then be restored and glorious (see Joshua 13:1–8; Isaiah 44:26).

9–10. THE PRISONERS . . . THOSE WHO ARE IN DARKNESS: At the Messiah's Second Advent, Israel's condition will change from captivity and oppression to contentment and prosperity, such as that enjoyed by a well-fed, protected, and watered flock of sheep. These ideal conditions will be enjoyed by the faithful remnant returning for their kingdom in Israel.

12. COME FROM AFAR: Israel's regathering will be from a worldwide exile, even faraway places like Sinim, which was probably an ancient name for what is now China.

GOD WILL REMEMBER ZION: *In this next section, Isaiah summarizes the nation's history of lament during its long period of suffering.*

16. INSCRIBED: The Lord is referring to the Jews' custom (perhaps drawn from Exodus 13), of puncturing their hands with a symbol of their city and temple as a sign of devotion.

18. BIND THEM ON YOU: Zion's sons will return as the city's destroyers depart and will adorn the city. Israel will be the means of the conversion of the nations in the end.

19. EVEN NOW BE TOO SMALL: After the faithful remnant is regathered in salvation and the Gentiles come to faith in the kingdom through Jewish witnesses, millennial Jerusalem will not be large enough to contain all her inhabitants.

22. AN OATH TO THE NATIONS: This promise will find literal fulfillment as the nations of the world assist the faithful remnant of Israel to return to their land. At the outset of the kingdom when this regathering takes place, all the Gentiles will be believers in Jesus who, by faith, escaped the wrath of the Lamb on the Day of the Lord and entered the kingdom. Nations and leaders that have oppressed Israel will humble themselves before the redeemed people of God's covenant, and Israel will know that waiting on the Lord will not disappoint.

24. SHALL THE PREY BE TAKEN: As in verse 14, Isaiah speaks of Zion again, expressing her despondency over her captivity and wondering about deliverance.

25. THUS SAYS THE LORD: The Lord replies again with these encouraging words. The strong language used in this section against Israel's enemies reassures her of eventual deliverance from her exile. In the book of Revelation, the angel of the waters draws on this terminology in celebrating the third bowl judgment (see 16:6). The destruction of Israel's enemies, led by Satan in the Tribulation, also fulfills this pledge.

26. ALL FLESH SHALL KNOW: God's deliverance of Israel will be so dramatic that the world will recognize that the Lord, the Savior, Redeemer, and Mighty One of Israel, is the true God.

50:1. CERTIFICATE OF YOUR MOTHER'S DIVORCE: Although the sufferings of Judah were the necessary result of sin, no certificate of divorce or sale to creditors occurred because Zion's separation from the Lord was only temporary. In fact, God gave the non-Davidic northern kingdom a certificate of divorce, but the unconditional promises of the Davidic Covenant precluded such a divorce for Judah, although there would be a time of separation.

2. WHY: God asks why no one was willing to believe and obey Him, even after everyone had seen His redemptive power in Egypt when He dried up the Red Sea (see Exodus 14:21), opened the river Jordan by turning it into dry land

(see Joshua 4:23), and killed the fish in Egypt (see Exodus 7:18–21). The Lord's power to redeem was indisputable.

> *THE THIRD SONG: The third of four Servant Songs is the Messiah's soliloquy about being perfected through obedience and sufferings.*

6. MY BACK ... MY CHEEKS ... MY FACE: The Servant remained obedient, though provoked to rebel by excessively vile treatment. Jesus fulfilled this prophecy by remaining submissive to the Father's will (see Matthew 26:67; Mark 14:65; Luke 22:63; John 18:22).

7. SET MY FACE LIKE A FLINT: So sure was the Servant of God's help that He resolutely determined to remain unswayed by whatever hardship might await Him. Jesus demonstrated this determination in setting His face to go to Jerusalem to be crucified (see Luke 9:51).

8–9. MY ADVERSARY: No matter how the Servant was mistreated, mocked, or repudiated, He had such full confidence of the Lord's support that He welcomed an adversary to come.

10–11. WHO AMONG YOU FEARS THE LORD?: What follows is a call to the unconverted to believe and be saved, along with a warning that those who tried to escape spiritual darkness by lighting their own fire (man-made religion, works righteousness) were to end up in eternal torment.

Read Isaiah 52:1–53:12, noting the key words and phrases indicated below.

> *GOD'S REDEMPTION: A call is now given for Zion to awake from her spiritual drunkenness and clothe herself in garments of honor and dignity.*

52:1–3. THE UNCLEAN SHALL NO LONGER COME TO YOU: Foreign invaders will no longer control the city at the time of her final restoration.

3. SOLD YOURSELVES FOR NOTHING ... REDEEMED WITHOUT MONEY: The Jews became the servants of their foreign conquerors, who paid nothing for Israel, so the Lord will redeem Israel gratuitously from sin.

5. THOSE WHO RULE: A reference to the Babylonians and their cruelty to captive Israelites.

MY NAME IS BLASPHEMED: Foreign rulers despised the God of Israel as long as His people were in bondage. God delivered His people, not for their goodness, but for the sake of His holy name—to prove He was truthful, faithful, and powerful. Paul later cited the blasphemy to Israel's God that resulted from the hypocrisy of first-century Jews not applying to themselves the standards of God that they knew and taught others (see Romans 2:24).

6. IN THAT DAY THAT I AM HE: After the Day of the Lord, when Israel experiences deliverance from her worldwide dispersion, she will recognize the fulfillment of prophecies through Isaiah and others and enjoy full assurance that the Lord had spoken and fulfilled His promises of deliverance. They will connect these events with the great "I AM."

7. HOW BEAUTIFUL . . . GOOD NEWS: Messengers will traverse the mountains around Jerusalem to spread the good news of the return of redeemed Israel to the land. Paul broadened this millennial reference to include spreading the gospel of God's grace from the time of Jesus Christ on (see Romans 10:15).

YOUR GOD REIGNS: The good news pertains to the ideal conditions of Israel's golden age, during which Christ will reign personally over His kingdom.

8. EYE TO EYE: This Hebrew expression portrayed two people so close together that they can look into each other's eyes. The point is that the messengers of the truth ("watchmen") will see the Lord return to Zion (a better translation) as vividly as they see each other eye to eye.

9–10. THE LORD HAS COMFORTED HIS PEOPLE: The ruined city will respond to the call to sing for joy because the Lord has provided comfort and redemption.

11. DEPART! DEPART!: The prophet commands the Israelites to leave the lands of their exiles to return to Jerusalem. Under Cyrus, there was only a limited return (numbering 50,000), but the final fulfillment in view here is in the future.

TOUCH NO UNCLEAN THING: The returning exiles were not to defile themselves by taking property home from their exile. The New Testament authors gave these prophetic words an application in principle by using them as an exhortation forbidding Christians to involve themselves with spiritual ties to forces of paganism (see 2 Corinthians 6:17).

12. NOT GO OUT WITH HASTE: The delivered captives will not have to hurry in their return to Jerusalem, as their ancestors did when delivered from

Egypt (see Exodus 12:11, 33, 39. They can move deliberately and safely, with the Messiah in front and God in back.

> THE FINAL SONG: *This last and most memorable of the four Servant Songs contains unarguable and incontrovertible proof that God is the author of Scripture and Jesus the fulfillment of messianic prophecy.*

13. BEHOLD, MY SERVANT SHALL DEAL PRUDENTLY: This final Servant Song contains unarguable, incontrovertible proof that God is the author of Scripture and Jesus the fulfillment of messianic prophecy. The details are so minute that no human could have predicted them by accident and no imposter could have fulfilled them by cunning. Clearly, this refers to Messiah Jesus, as the New Testament attests (see Matthew 8:17; Mark 15:28; Luke 22:37; John 12:38). It is often alluded to without being quoted (see Mark 9:12; Romans 4:25; 1 Peter 1:19; 1 John 3:5).

EXALTED AND EXTOLLED: Ultimately, when the Servant rules over His kingdom, He will receive international recognition for the effectiveness of His reign.

14. HIS VISAGE WAS MARRED: The Servant must undergo inhuman cruelty to the point that He no longer looks like a human being. His appearance is so awful that people look at Him in astonishment (see Matthew 26:67; 27:30; John 19:3).

15. SPRINKLE MANY NATIONS: In His disfigured state, the Servant will perform a priestly work of cleansing not just Israel but many people outside the nation.

SHUT THEIR MOUTHS: At His exaltation, human leaders in the highest places will be speechless and in awe before the once-despised Servant. When He takes His throne, they will see the unfolding of power and glory such as they have never imagined.

53:1. WHO HAS BELIEVED OUR REPORT?: The question implies that, in spite of these and other prophecies, only a few would recognize the Servant when He appeared. This anticipation found literal fulfillment at Christ's First Advent, when Israel did not welcome Him (see John 1:9–11; 12:38). Paul applied the same prophecy to the world at large (see Romans 10:16).

THE ARM OF THE LORD: At His First Coming, the nation did not recognize the mighty, incarnate power of God in the person of Jesus, their Deliverer.

2. BEFORE HIM: Though unrecognized by the world, Jesus was observed carefully by God, who ordered every minute circumstance of His life.

NO BEAUTY: The Servant would arise in lowly conditions and wear none of the usual emblems of royalty, making His true identity visible only to the discerning eye of faith.

3. DESPISED AND REJECTED: The prophet foresees the hatred and rejection by mankind toward the Messiah/Servant, who suffered not only external abuse but also internal grief over the lack of response from those He came to save (see Matthew 23:37; Luke 13:34).

WE HID . . . WE DID NOT ESTEEM HIM: By using the first person, the prophet spoke for his unbelieving nation's aversion to a crucified Messiah and their lack of respect for the incarnate Son of God.

4. BORNE OUR GRIEFS . . . CARRIED OUR SORROWS: Even though the verbs are past tense, they predict happenings future to Isaiah's time. Isaiah was saying the Messiah would bear the consequences of the sins of men, namely the griefs and sorrows of life, though incredibly, the Jews who watched Him die thought He was being punished by God for His own sins. Matthew found an analogical fulfillment of these words in Jesus' healing ministry, because sickness results from sin for which the Servant paid with His life. In eternity, all sickness will be removed, so ultimately healing is included in the benefits of the atonement.

5. WOUNDED FOR OUR TRANSGRESSIONS . . . BRUISED FOR OUR INIQUITIES: This verse is filled with the language of substitution. The Servant would suffer not for His own sin, since He would be sinless, but as the substitute for sinners. The emphasis here is on Christ being the substitute recipient of God's wrath on sinners (see 2 Corinthians 5:21; Galatians 1:3–4; Hebrews 10:9–10).

CHASTISEMENT FOR OUR PEACE: The Servant would suffer the chastisement of God in order to procure the believer's peace with God.

BY HIS STRIPES WE ARE HEALED: The stripe (the Hebrew noun is singular) that caused the Servant's death has brought salvation to those for whose sins He died.

6. ALL WE . . . EVERY ONE . . . US ALL: Every person has sinned, but the Servant has sufficiently shouldered the consequences of sin and the righteous

wrath deserved by elect sinners. The manner in which God laid our iniquity on Him was that God treated Him as if He had committed every sin ever committed by every person who would ever believe, though He was perfectly innocent of any sin. God did so to Him so that, God's wrath being spent and justice satisfied, He could then give to the account of sinners who believe, the righteousness of Christ, treating them as if they had done only the righteous acts of Christ. In both cases, this is substitution.

7. OPENED NOT HIS MOUTH: The Servant will utter no protest and will be utterly submissive to those who oppress Him. Jesus fulfilled this prophecy (see Matthew 26:63; 27:12–14; Mark 14:61; 15:5; Luke 23:9; John 19:9; 1 Peter 2:23).

LAMB TO THE SLAUGHTER: The Servant was to assume the role of a sacrificial lamb. Jesus literally fulfilled this figurative role (see John 1:29; 1 Peter 1:18–19; Revelation 5:6).

8. CUT OFF . . . FOR THE TRANSGRESSIONS OF MY PEOPLE: The Servant lost His life so He could be the substitute object of wrath in the place of the Jews, who by that substitution will receive salvation and the righteousness of God imputed to them.

9. WITH THE WICKED . . . WITH THE RICH AT HIS DEATH: Because of the Servant's ignominious death, the Jews intended Him to have a disgraceful burial along with the thieves, but instead He was buried with "the rich" in an honorable burial, through the donated tomb of wealthy Joseph of Arimathea (see Matthew 27:57–60; Mark 15:42–46; Luke 23:50–53; John 19:38–40).

NO VIOLENCE, NOR . . . DECEIT: The Servant's innocence meant that His execution was totally undeserved. Peter notes the fulfillment of this prophecy in Christ (see 1 Peter 2:22).

10. IT PLEASED THE LORD: Although the Servant did not deserve to die, it was the Lord's will for Him to do so (see Matthew 26:39; Luke 22:42; John 12:27; Acts 2:23).

AN OFFERING FOR SIN: This was fulfilled by the Servant as the lamb of God (see verse 7; John 1:29). Jesus is the Christian's Passover (see 1 Corinthians 5:7). This conclusively eliminates the error that Christ's atonement provides present-day healing for those who pray in faith. His death was an atonement for sin, not sickness.

SEE HIS SEED . . . PROLONG HIS DAYS: To see His seed, the Servant must rise from the dead. He would do this and live to reign forever.

11. HE SHALL . . . BE SATISFIED: The one sacrifice of the Servant will provide complete satisfaction in settling the sin issue (see 1 John 2:2).

BY HIS KNOWLEDGE: The Servant knew exactly what needed to be done to solve the sin problem.

JUSTIFY MANY: Through the divine "knowledge" of how to justify sinners, the plan was so accomplished that by Messiah's one sacrifice, He declared many righteous before God (see Romans 5:19; 2 Corinthians 5:21).

12. PORTION WITH THE GREAT . . . SPOIL WITH THE STRONG: The Servant's reward for His work will be to enjoy the "spoils" of His spiritual victories during His millennial reign.

NUMBERED WITH THE TRANSGRESSORS: The Servant would assume a role among sinful human beings, fulfilled by Jesus when He was crucified between two criminals (see Luke 22:37).

MADE INTERCESSION FOR THE TRANSGRESSORS: This speaks of the office of intercessory High Priest, which began on the cross and continues in heaven (see Luke 23:34; Hebrews 7:25; 9:24).

UNLEASHING THE TEXT

1) How does the second Servant Song (49:1–13) point forward to the life and ministry of Jesus?

_____

_____

_____

_____

_____

_____

2) Why did God's people need to endure a period of suffering and separation from Him? Why was that separation temporary?

_____

_____

_____

_____

_____

_____

3) What details do you find most striking from the final Servant Song (52:13–53:12)? Why?

_____

_____

_____

_____

_____

_____

4) What can we learn about Jesus from that final song?

_____

_____

_____

_____

EXPLORING THE MEANING

Salvation is for all people. One of the areas of confusion that often led to sinful pride for the Israelites—both in Isaiah's time and beyond—was their unique relationship with God as His chosen people. Many residents of Israel and Judah believed that they had an exclusionary connection with God, and that God would always and only operate with their best national interests in mind, with no consideration of other peoples except to execute judgment over them.

In reality, God's selection of the Jewish people was always intended as the vehicle through which He would reveal Himself to the entire world. Even as far back as God's call to Abraham, this purpose was clear: "Now the LORD had said to Abram: 'Get out of your country, from your family and from your father's house, to a land that I will show you. I will make you a great nation; I will bless you and make your name great; and you shall be a blessing. I will bless those who bless you, and I will curse him who curses you; and *in you all the families of the earth shall be blessed*'" (Genesis 12:1–3, emphasis added).

God confirmed this plan in the second Servant Song when He declared through Isaiah, "It is too small a thing that You should be My Servant to raise up the tribes of Jacob, and to restore the preserved ones of Israel; I will also give You as a light to the Gentiles, that You should be My salvation to the ends of the earth" (Isaiah 49:6). In eternity past, God chose to save sinners from every nation and people group. His gift of salvation was made possible only through the death and resurrection of Jesus Christ.

Salvation requires a substitutionary atonement. Many Bible readers mistakenly believe salvation to be an exclusively New Testament concept. In truth, many of the key doctrines that lay the foundation for our understanding of salvation are sown throughout the Old Testament. This includes the doctrine of *substitutionary atonement*. As an example, look at these verses from Isaiah 53:

> Surely He has borne our griefs
> And carried our sorrows;
> Yet we esteemed Him stricken,
> Smitten by God, and afflicted.
> But He was wounded for our transgressions,
> He was bruised for our iniquities;
> The chastisement for our peace was upon Him,
> And by His stripes we are healed (verses 4–5).

These verses point forward 700 years from Isaiah's time to give a picture of Jesus' crucifixion. They vividly illustrate how Christ would provide atonement for the sins of those He chose to save. For believers, Christ has "borne our griefs" and "carried our sorrows." He was "wounded for our transgressions" and bruised not for *His* iniquities, but for *ours*. Isaiah prophetically explains that Jesus would endure the punishment for sin on our behalf, explaining that "by His stripes we are healed."

The reality of our fallen state is that all of us have sinned, and the wages of that sin is death (see Romans 3:23; 6:23). Yet, as we discover in this final Servant Song, God always intended for the Messiah to bear the punishment for sin so that all who trust in Him could be saved.

God's Word is trustworthy. As we read through the dramatic prophecies about Jesus in the Servant Songs of Isaiah, it is important to take a step back and reflect on the supernatural origin of those prophecies. Isaiah lived and ministered centuries years before the birth of Christ. Yet the accuracy and detailed specificity of his words are staggering. For example, in Isaiah 49, the prophet declares that Jesus would be "formed" in His mother's womb (verse 5)—meaning He would be born as a human being. (It is further clarified in Isaiah 7:14 that Jesus would be born of a virgin.)

Regarding the crucifixion, Isaiah's prophecies in chapter 53 are especially striking. Isaiah also declared, "As a sheep before its shearers is silent, so He opened not His mouth" (Isaiah 53:7). This was fulfilled by Jesus' refusal to defend Himself in front of the Sanhedrin and Pontius Pilate. Finally, Isaiah prophesied, "And they made His grave with the wicked—but with the rich at His death" (verse 9). The Jewish leaders of Jesus' day desired to crucify and bury Jesus as a criminal, yet Christ was placed in the tomb of Joseph of Arimathea, a rich man (see Matthew 27:57–60).

The book of Isaiah contains dozens of prophecies about Jesus that He fulfilled in His lifetime. The details are so minute that no human could have predicted them by accident and no imposter fulfilled them by cunning. God wove such specificity into Isaiah's prophecy as a testimony to His sovereignty, and to unmistakably identify His Son as the long-awaited Messiah.

REFLECTING ON THE TEXT

5) Christ's redeeming work isn't limited by ethnic or social boundaries. What impact does that have in calling others to repentance and faith?

_____
_____
_____
_____
_____
_____

6) What can we learn about God from the doctrine of substitutionary atonement?

_____
_____
_____
_____
_____

7) If you are a believer, Christ bore your punishment on the cross. How does that affect the way you think about temptation and sin?

_____

_____

_____

_____

_____

8) How does Christ's fulfilment of the prophecies in Isaiah 53 affirm and defend the authority and inerrancy of God's Word?

_____

_____

_____

_____

_____

PERSONAL RESPONSE

9) What steps can you take this week to help bring the gospel message to all people?

_____

_____

_____

_____

10) What are some ways you can express your thanks and appreciation to Jesus for all He has done for you?

_____

_____

_____

_____

10

REDEMPTION THROUGH THE SERVANT
Isaiah 54:1–57:14

DRAWING NEAR

_____

_____

_____

_____

_____

_____

_____

_____

_____

THE CONTEXT

As we have seen, the first half of Isaiah's prophecy (through chapter 39) focuses primarily on God's judgments spoken against Israel, Judah, and the surrounding nations. Beginning with chapter 40, however, Isaiah's prophecy shifts to deal with promises of God's healing, blessing, and restoration after those periods of judgment take place.

In the previous lessons, we examined how many of those blessings would be dependent on the work of God's Servant, the Messiah. In the four Servant Songs of Isaiah, we learn much about God's anointing of Jesus and His mission and ministry in the world. These include His sacrificial death as God's solely satisfactory method of providing atonement.

In this lesson, we will gain a further picture of the results achieved through Jesus' life, death, and resurrection. Specifically, we will explore the principle of redemption. Importantly, the promises described in these chapters in Isaiah were not given only to God's chosen people, the Jews, but also to all nations and all peoples who would believe.

KEYS TO THE TEXT

Read Isaiah 54:1–57:21, noting the key words and phrases indicated below.

> PEACE AND ABUNDANT LIFE: *God's people will receive many blessings through the work and ministry of the Messiah.*

54:1. O BARREN, YOU WHO HAVE NOT BORNE: In her exile and dispersion, Israel has been destitute and disgraced, as a woman who had borne no children. The prophet calls for singing, however, because of the Lord's promise of future fruitfulness for the nation. In the New Testament, the apostle Paul supplies an additional application of the principle in this verse, citing it as evidence that the Jerusalem above, mother of the children of promise through Sarah, will enjoy great fruitfulness. "For it is written: 'Rejoice, O barren, you who do not bear! Break forth and shout, you who are not in labor! For the desolate has many more children than she who has a husband'" (Galatians 4:27).

2. ENLARGE THE PLACE OF YOUR TENT: The prophet commands barren Israel to prepare for the day when her numerous inhabitants will require a larger space in which to dwell.

3. YOUR DESCENDANTS WILL INHERIT THE NATIONS: The Messiah's future kingdom is to be worldwide, far greater in extent than the former kingdoms of David and Solomon.

4. YOU WILL FORGET THE SHAME OF YOUR YOUTH: Israel's sins brought on the Egyptian captivity, the Babylonian exile, and her current dispersion, but the glories of the future kingdom will be so great they will overshadow past failures.

5. YOUR MAKER IS YOUR HUSBAND . . . AND YOUR REDEEMER: The basis for forgetting past failures is Israel's relationship to the Lord as her husband and Redeemer.

6. LIKE A WOMAN FORSAKEN AND GRIEVED . . . REFUSED: Israel in exile and dispersion has been like a wife whose husband has rejected her. But this

is only for a brief time, as compared to the everlasting kindness she will enjoy when the Messiah returns to gather the woeful wife.

9. WATERS OF NOAH: God swore that He would never again judge the whole earth with a flood. "Then the LORD said in His heart, 'I will never again curse the ground for man's sake, although the imagination of man's heart is evil from his youth; nor will I again destroy every living thing as I have done'" (Genesis 8:21). In the same way, He has taken an oath never to be angry with His people again. He will fulfill this promise after their final restoration.

10. THE MOUNTAINS . . . AND THE HILLS BE REMOVED . . . MY KIND- NESS SHALL NOT DEPART . . . MY COVENANT: During the Millennium, the topography will change. "The mountains will melt under Him, and the valleys will split like wax before the fire, like waters poured down a steep place" (Micah 1:4; see also Ezekiel 38:20; Zechariah 14:4, 10). However, God's pledge of well-being for Israel as a result of the New Covenant will never change.

11–12. COLORFUL GEMS . . . SAPPHIRES . . . RUBIES . . . CRYSTAL . . . PRECIOUS STONES: The elaborate ornamentation will outfit the new Jerusalem to be the center of the future, eternal messianic reign following the Millennium. As John later wrote, "The foundations of the wall of the city were adorned with all kinds of precious stones: the first foundation was jasper, the second sapphire, the third chalcedony, the fourth emerald, the fifth sardonyx, the sixth sardius, the seventh chrysolite, the eighth beryl, the ninth topaz, the tenth chrysoprase, the eleventh jacinth, and the twelfth amethyst" (Revelation 21:19–20).

13. YOUR CHILDREN SHALL BE TAUGHT BY THE LORD: As magnificent as this ornamentation will be in the new Jerusalem, it is not as important as the spiritual richness of the kingdom, when truth and peace prevail along with righteousness. The Lord Himself will teach everyone during the messianic king-dom, so everyone will know His righteousness. Jesus gave this verse an addi-tional focus, applying it to those with spiritual insight who would come to Him during His First Advent. "It is written in the prophets, 'And they shall all be taught by God.' Therefore everyone who has heard and learned from the Father comes to Me" (John 6:45).

15. WHOEVER ASSEMBLES AGAINST YOU SHALL FALL: This will occur in the millennial kingdom as prophesied by John in Revelation 20:7–9. The Lord will burn up all of Israel's enemies. The heritage of the Lord's servants in the Messiah's kingdom will include His protection from would-be

conquerors. It should be noted that after the Servant Song of Isaiah 53, Israel is for the rest of Isaiah's book always referred to as God's "servants" (plural) rather than His servant.

> AN INVITATION TO ALL: *The prophet invites his readers to participate in all the benefits obtained by the suffering of the Servant.*

55:1. EVERYONE WHO THIRSTS: The Servant's redemptive work and glorious kingdom are for the benefit of all who are willing to come.

WITHOUT MONEY AND WITHOUT PRICE: Benefits in the Servant's kingdom will be free because of His redemptive work. As Paul later wrote, "For by grace you have been saved through faith, and that not of yourselves; it is the gift of God, not of works, lest anyone should boast" (Ephesians 2:8–9).

WINE AND MILK: These are symbols for abundance, satisfaction, and prosperity. "And it will come to pass in that day that the mountains shall drip with new wine, the hills shall flow with milk, and all the brooks of Judah shall be flooded with water" (Joel 3:18).

2. WHAT IS NOT BREAD: This is the "bread of deceit" (Proverbs 20:17) and not the "bread of life" that is Christ (John 6:35).

3. I WILL MAKE AN EVERLASTING COVENANT: The New Covenant that God will give to Israel. "Behold, the days are coming, says the LORD, when I will make a new covenant with the house of Israel and with the house of Judah—not according to the covenant that I made with their fathers in the day that I took them by the hand to lead them out of the land of Egypt, My covenant which they broke, though I was a husband to them, says the Lord. But this is the covenant that I will make with the house of Israel after those days, says the LORD: I will put My law in their minds, and write it on their hearts; and I will be their God, and they shall be My people. No more shall every man teach his neighbor, and every man his brother, saying, 'Know the LORD,' for they all shall know Me, from the least of them to the greats of them, says the LORD. For I will forgive their iniquity, and their sin I will remember no more." (Jeremiah 31:31–34).

SURE MERCIES OF DAVID: The Davidic Covenant promised David that from his seed would be a ruler over Israel in an everlasting kingdom (see 2 Samuel 7:8, 16). Paul connected the resurrection of Christ with this promise, since it was an essential event in fulfilling this promise. "He raised Him from the dead, no more to return to corruption, He has spoken thus: 'I will give you the sure mercies of David'" (Acts 13:34).

4. A LEADER AND COMMANDER: If Christ had not fully satisfied God by His atoning death, He would not have risen. And if He had not risen from the dead, He could not eventually sit on David's earthly throne. But He did rise and will fulfill the kingly role; the whole world will come to Him as the Great King.

6. SEEK THE LORD WHILE HE MAY BE FOUND: Here is one of the clearest invitations in the Old Testament to salvation now and kingdom blessing later. It gives an excellent example of how people were saved during the Old Testament period. Salvation grace and mercy were available to the soul who was willing to (1) seek the Lord, and (2) call on Him while He is still available. "For He says: 'In an acceptable time I have heard you, and in the day of salvation I have helped you.' Behold, now is the accepted time; behold, now is the day of salvation" (2 Corinthians 6:2).

7. LET THE WICKED FORSAKE HIS WAY: Such true, seeking in faith is always accompanied by repentance, an integral part of seeking the Lord, which is described as forsaking ungodly ways and thoughts and turning from sinful living to the Lord. A sinner must come believing in God, recognizing his sin, and desiring forgiveness and deliverance from that sin. At the same time, he must recognize his own inability to be righteous or to satisfy God, and cast himself on God's mercy. It is then that he receives a complete pardon. His sin has been covered by the substitution of the Messiah in his place. (This Old Testament pattern of salvation is illustrated in Luke 18:9–14.)

8. MY THOUGHTS ARE NOT YOUR THOUGHTS, NOR . . . MY WAYS: Some people may doubt such a willingness on the Lord's part to pardon sin. However, God's grace is far beyond human comprehension, especially as manifested toward Israel.

10. AS THE RAIN . . . SNOW . . . SO SHALL MY WORD: Moisture from heaven invariably accomplishes its intended purpose in helping meet human physical needs. The Word of God will likewise produce its intended results in fulfilling God's spiritual purposes, especially the establishment of the Davidic kingdom on earth.

12. YOU SHALL GO OUT WITH JOY, AND BE LED OUT WITH PEACE: Exiled Israel will return from her dispersion rejoicing in her deliverance and unbothered by her enemies.

13. INSTEAD OF THE THORN . . . MYRTLE TREE: In the Davidic kingdom, positive changes in nature, including the reverse of the curse, will be an ongoing testimony to the Lord's redemption of His people. "The creation was subjected to futility, not willingly, but because of Him who subjected it in hope; because the creation itself also will be delivered from the bondage of corruption into the glorious liberty of the children of God" (Romans 8:20–21).

SALVATION AND HEALING: THE Messiah's work will bring salvation to all people, including healing for those who turn away from their rebellion against God.

56:1. ABOUT TO COME . . . TO BE REVEALED: Incentives to comply with seeking the Lord, calling upon His name, forsaking wickedness, and returning to the Lord (see verses 6–7) include the nearness of God's kingdom of salvation and righteousness.

2. KEEPS FROM DEFILING THE SABBATH: Sabbath observance, established after the deliverance from Egypt, became a sign of fulfilling the covenant God made with Moses.

3. THE FOREIGNER . . . THE EUNUCH: Such individuals, excluded from Israel by the law, will find in the coming of the messianic kingdom the removal of such exclusions. Eunuchs with hearts inclined to comply with the Mosaic covenant may anticipate an endless posterity.

4–5. HOLD FAST MY COVENANT: Works can never save a person. Rather, obeying God's Law, doing what pleases Him, and desiring to keep the promises of obedience are the evidences that one has been saved and will, thus, enjoy all salvation blessings. As Paul later wrote, "For by grace you have been saved through faith, and that not of yourselves; it is the gift of God, not of works, lest anyone should boast" (Ephesians 2:8–9).

6–7. ACCEPTED ON MY ALTAR: The foreigner who loves God, whose heart is inclined to serve Him, and who obeys the Mosaic Law, will find his sacrifices welcome in the coming kingdom as well.

7. MY HOUSE . . . FOR ALL NATIONS: In the kingdom of the Messiah, the Jerusalem temple will be the focal point for worship of the Lord by people of all ethnic backgrounds. Jesus cited a violation of this anticipation by His contemporaries in His second cleansing of the temple: The Jewish leaders had made the temple

a commercial venture. "He said to them, 'It is written, "My house shall be called a house of prayer," but you have made it a "den of thieves""'" (Matthew 21:13).

8. OTHERS BESIDES THOSE WHO ARE GATHERED TO HIM: In addition to gathering Israel's exiles into His kingdom, the Lord will bring in non-Jews as well.

ISRAEL'S FALSE LEADERS: Isaiah provides a commentary on Israel's false prophets and irresponsible leaders who led them astray and into idolatry.

9. YOU BEASTS OF THE FIELD: Isaiah uses the terms "beasts," "watchmen," and "shepherds" here to identify the wicked. Other prophets also refer to Israel's enemies as beasts (see, for example, Jeremiah 12:9; Ezekiel 34:5, 8). Prophets, who should have been watchmen and should have warned Israel to repent, ignored their responsibility (see Ezekiel 3:17). Priests also failed to lead Israel in paths of righteousness (see Ezekiel 34:1–6).

12. I WILL BRING WINE: This is indicative of the self-indulgent irresponsibility of the leaders. Drunkenness obliterated any concern that they had for their people.

57:1–2. THE RIGHTEOUS PERISHES: In contrast to the evil leaders, who were engaged in debauchery and self-indulgence, were the righteous who were removed from impending divine judgments. The righteous do suffer by oppression and distress at what is going on around them, but they die in faith and enjoy their eternal reward.

3. SONS OF THE SORCERESS . . . OFFSPRING OF THE ADULTERER: Sorcery and adultery were figurative designations for idolatry. God summoned the wicked to give an account.

4. AND STICK OUT THE TONGUE?: The ungodly blatantly ridiculed God's messengers.

5–6. SLAYING THE CHILDREN: Isaiah here describes elements of idolatry such as child sacrifice, which were a part of worshiping the Ammonite god Molech. In response to Israel's offerings to idols, what was the Lord's appropriate response—to be satisfied or to take vengeance? Jeremiah had the answer: "'Shall I not punish them for these things?' says the LORD. 'And shall I not avenge Myself on such a nation as this?'" (Jeremiah 5:9, 29; 9:9).

7–8. ON A LOFTY AND HIGH MOUNTAIN: The locations of idol altars, where Israel committed spiritual adultery in offering sacrifices to Baal and Astarte.

9. WENT TO THE KING: An example of this was Ahaz, who called on the king of Assyria for help and spared no expense in copying that nation's idolatry (see 2 Kings 16:7–18).

10. FOUND THE LIFE OF YOUR HAND: Rather than recognizing the hopelessness of idolatry, and in spite of the weariness of idol worship, the Israelites found renewed strength to pursue their idolatrous course.

11. YOU HAVE LIED: These wicked people feared false gods more than the true God to whom they played the hypocrite, trading on God's patience.

12–13. I WILL DECLARE YOUR RIGHTEOUSNESS: God will break His silence by elaborating on Israel's sham righteousness—a sarcastic way of saying they have no real righteousness. The folly of such devotion to nonexistent gods will show up when judgment comes and all of them are blown away, while the worshipers of the true God enjoy the blessings of the kingdom.

> *A PROMISE OF HEALING: In contrast to the threats of judgment for idolatry that Isaiah has just related, here God provides promises of blessing.*

14. TAKE THE STUMBLING BLOCK: The command is to remove all barriers in order to prepare the way for God's people to return to Him.

15, 18. REVIVE THE SPIRIT OF THE HUMBLE: The Lord sends true revival, which comes to the humble and contrite. After all the years of Israel's sin, backsliding, and punishment, God's grace will prevail, and spiritual healing and restoration will come.

19. FRUIT OF THE LIPS: According to the author of Hebrews, this phrase refers to praising and thanking God. "Therefore by Him let us continually offer the sacrifice of praise to God, that is, the fruit of our lips, giving thanks to His name" (Hebrews 13:15). In this context in Isaiah, it is the voice crying, "peace, peace," in a call to people far and near to come to the Lord and receive spiritual healing.

20. LIKE THE TROUBLED SEA: In contrast to those people just named, who seek the Lord, the wicked enjoy anything but peace.

UNLEASHING THE TEXT

1) What does it mean that God is our Redeemer?

_____

_____

_____

2) How are God's thoughts and ways unlike those of men? Be specific.

_____

_____

_____

3) Prior to Christ's atoning death, how were Old Testament saints saved?

_____

_____

_____

4) How do the promises described in these chapters inform the way you share the gospel with others?

_____

_____

_____

_____

EXPLORING THE MEANING

God is our Redeemer. In Isaiah 54, God warned that His people would go through times of trial and difficulty. Those trials were the direct result of their sin and rejection of Him. Even so, God promised that His people could look forward to a future period of restoration and healing. And in describing those future realities, God used an interesting term to describe Himself: *Redeemer*. "For your Maker is your husband," He proclaimed, "The LORD of hosts is His name; and your Redeemer is the Holy One of Israel" (verse 5). Later, He added, "'With a little

135

wrath I hid My face from you for a moment; but with everlasting kindness I will have mercy on you,' says the LORD, your Redeemer" (verse 8).

In the ancient world, to *redeem* something was a legal and financial endeavor. It meant paying a specified price in order to restore something that had been lost or that had gone into default. As an example, it was common in Israelite society for people to sell themselves as servants or slaves when they endured financial difficulty or were unable to pay a debt. In such situations, that person's family member could step in and pay a price to "redeem" the struggling person and end his or her slavery (see Leviticus 25:25). Similarly, God required His people to sacrifice the firstborn of any animal as an offering to Him. However, they could "redeem" the firstborn of a donkey—a valuable animal— by offering a lamb instead.

As we saw in Isaiah 53, Jesus the Messiah offered Himself on the cross to take the punishment for our sin. Thus, He redeemed us and purchased our salvation by paying the price we were unable to pay.

Repentance is a key element of salvation. Jesus' death on the cross paid the price for the sins of those God chose to save. Scripture makes it clear that salvation is God's work alone—that we are saved by grace through faith (Ephesians 2:8–9). The outward manifestation of that inward transformation is called repentance.

Again, while many Bible readers think of repentance as a New Testament concept, we find a call to repent in chapter 55 of Isaiah's prophecy: "Seek the LORD while He may be found, call upon Him while He is near. Let the wicked forsake his way, and the unrighteous man his thoughts; let him return to the LORD, and He will have mercy on him; and to our God, for He will abundantly pardon" (verses 6–7). As new creations in Christ, we repudiate the sin and corruption that once dominated our lives, and long for righteousness.

In Luke's gospel, Jesus provides us with a vivid illustration of the difference between empty professions of faith and true repentance. "Two men went up to the temple to pray, one a Pharisee and the other a tax collector. The Pharisee stood and prayed thus with himself, 'God, I thank You that I am not like other men— extortioners, unjust, adulterers, or even as this tax collector. I fast twice a week; I give tithes of all that I possess.' And the tax collector, standing afar off, would not so much as raise his eyes to heaven, but beat his breast, saying, 'God, be merciful to me a sinner!'"(Luke 18:10–13). In faith, we cling to the atoning work of Christ. In repentance, we reject and turn from the sinful lives that incurred the penalty He alone could pay.

Redemption is a limited-time offer. The end of Isaiah 57 is a poignant call from God to His people, Israel, reminding them to repent and return to Him. God told His people, "I dwell in the high and holy place, with him who has a contrite and humble spirit, to revive the spirit of the humble" (verse 15). Despite the "backsliding" (verse 17) of His people, God declared, "I have seen his ways, and will heal him; I will also lead him, and restore comforts to him and to his mourners" (verse 18).

We know from Scripture that a remnant of Israel will accept God's offer and return to Him through Jesus, the rightful Messiah (see Isaiah 10:20; Revelation 7:2–8). However, this passage is also a good reminder for all readers that God's offer of redemption is not available for an unlimited amount of time. Rather, we all must recognize our need for forgiveness and salvation, and turn to Him in faith before our lives come to an end on this side of eternity.

The author of Hebrews expressed this idea of a limited-time offer in stark terms: "And as it is appointed for men to die once, but after this the judgment, so Christ was offered once to bear the sins of many" (Hebrews 9:27). Death is a reality for every human being. Too often we forget that judgment after death is also a reality. In the words of Isaiah 55:6, we must "seek the LORD while He may be found."

REFLECTING ON THE TEXT

5) How would you explain the concept of redemption in your own words?

_____

_____

_____

_____

6) What are some specific ways you have repented of your sins?

_____

_____

_____

_____

7) What does repentance look like for those who God has saved?

_____

_____

_____

_____

_____

8) Why do we urgently call people to repent and believe on this side of eternity?

_____

_____

_____

_____

_____

PERSONAL RESPONSE

9) Where do you see opportunities for repentance in your life?

_____

_____

_____

_____

_____

10) Who are some unsaved friends and family members whose repentance you will pray for this week?

_____

_____

_____

_____

_____

THE FUTURE GLORY
OF GOD'S PEOPLE
Isaiah 58:1–14; 61:1–11; 63:1–64:12; 66:1–24

DRAWING NEAR

How does the promise of heaven and future glorification inform and animate how you live on this side of eternity?

_____

_____

_____

_____

_____

_____

_____

_____

_____

_____

THE CONTEXT

As we've seen throughout this study, time is a major factor when it comes to reading and understanding the book of Isaiah. The prophecies represent many different layers of time, and therefore point to many different audiences to whom God was speaking.

The first layer, of course, is the original hearers of Isaiah's prophecy—those residents of Judah and Jerusalem to whom Isaiah declared, "Hear the word of the

LORD" (Isaiah 1:10). A second layer includes Judah and Israel's contemporaries, the surrounding nations; Isaiah's prophecy included words of judgment against those nations, which would primarily be fulfilled in the immediate future. A third layer includes the then-future residents of Judah and Jerusalem who would endure the terror of the Babylonian conquest, yet who would ultimately experience God's healing. A fourth layer includes the first coming of Jesus, the Messiah, into the world. A final layer points to the Messiah's return and further events that remain to be fulfilled in the future, even for modern readers.

As we approach these final chapters of Isaiah's prophecy, we find the text alternating back and forth between the first and final layers. Isaiah speaks often about the leaders of his day, who ignored justice and allowed God's people to wander astray. He then also paints vivid pictures of the future glory to be experienced by God's people and reveals the many ways that God will bless those who faithfully follow Him.

KEYS TO THE TEXT

Read Isaiah 58:1–14, noting the key words and phrases indicated below.

> RETURN TO GOD: *God called on Israel to to repent of their spiritual infidelity. He illustrates the emptiness of the ritualism with two examples: fasting and observing the Sabbath.*

58:1. TELL MY PEOPLE THEIR TRANSGRESSION: Isaiah was to tell the people of Israel in plain language those areas of their behavior with which the Lord was displeased.

2. TAKE DELIGHT IN APPROACHING GOD: Israel was merely "going through the motions." Their appearance of righteousness was mere pretense.

3. WHY HAVE WE FASTED . . . AND YOU HAVE NOT SEEN?: The people complained when God did not recognize their religious actions, but God responds that their fastings have been only half-hearted. Hypocritical fasting resulted in contention, quarreling, and pretense, excluding the possibility of genuine prayer to God. Fasting consisted of more than just an outward ritual and a mock repentance. It involved penitence over sin and consequent humility, disconnecting from sin and oppression of others, feeding the hungry, and acting humanely toward those in need.

8. YOUR RIGHTEOUSNESS SHALL GO BEFORE YOU: When Israel learned the proper way to fast, she would enjoy the blessings of salvation and the Messiah's kingdom.

9. HERE I AM: A time will come when the Lord will be completely responsive to the prayers of His people. This will be done when they are converted and give evidence of that transformation in the kind of works that reflect a truly repentant heart. At the time of Christ's return, Israel will demonstrate true repentance, and the fullness of blessing will be poured out.

12. BUILD THE OLD WASTE PLACES: In view here is the final restoration of the millennial Jerusalem, of which Nehemiah's rebuilding of the walls was only a foretaste (see Nehemiah 2:17; Amos 9:11).

13. TURN AWAY YOUR FOOT FROM THE SABBATH: The Sabbath was holy ground on which no one should walk. Keeping the Sabbath was symbolic of obedience to all the law of Moses.

14. DELIGHT YOURSELF IN THE LORD: Repentant people walking in fellowship with the Lord experience satisfaction of soul. Their satisfaction will not come from material goods.

Read Isaiah 61:1–11, noting the key words and phrases indicated below.

THE ULTIMATE PREACHER AND REDEEMER: The prophet Isaiah now describes how the Servant of the Lord will be the ultimate Preacher and the Redeemer of Israel.

61:1 THE SPIRIT OF THE LORD GOD IS UPON ME: The three persons of the Holy Trinity function together in this verse. Jesus spoke of the initial fulfillment of this promise, referring it to His ministry of providing salvation's comfort to the spiritually oppressed (see Luke 4:18–19). Yet the Jews who were saved during Christ's ministry, and those being saved during this church age, still do not fulfill the promise of the salvation of the nation to come in the end time.

LIBERTY TO THE CAPTIVES: The "captives" are Israelites remaining in the dispersion following the Babylonian captivity.

2. ACCEPTABLE YEAR: The same as "the day of salvation" (Isaiah 49:8) and "the year of My redeemed" (63:4). This is where Jesus stopped reading in the

synagogue, indicating that the writing in the rest of this chapter awaited His Second Coming.

DAY OF VENGEANCE: As part of His deliverance of Israel, the Lord will pour out wrath on all who oppose Him (see Revelation 6–19).

3. CONSOLE THOSE WHO MOURN: The purpose of the Lord's consolation of the mourners after centuries of suffering will be to glorify Himself.

4. REBUILD THE OLD RUINS: The rebuilding of Israel's cities is part of God's future plan.

6. PRIESTS OF THE LORD: In fulfillment of Exodus 19:6, Israel will be a kingdom of priests when Christ establishes His kingdom. In the meantime, Peter applied the same terminology to the church (see 1 Peter 2:9).

7. DOUBLE HONOR: Israel will receive double portions of blessing to replace the double punishment of her exile (see Isaiah 40:2).

10. COVERED ME WITH THE ROBE OF RIGHTEOUSNESS: Here is the Old Testament picture of imputed righteousness, the essential heart of the New Covenant. When a sinner recognizes that he can't achieve his own righteousness by works, so that he repents and calls on the mercy of God, the Lord covers him with His own divine righteousness by grace through faith.

Read Isaiah 63:1–64:12, noting the key words and phrases indicated below.

JUDGMENT AND SALVATION: Isaiah speaks of God's future reckoning with the wicked and His compassionate acts toward Israel in spite of their unfaithfulness.

63:1. EDOM . . . BOZRAH: Edom represents a God-hating world, and here, specifically, the last and most bitter foes of God and His people. Bozrah was a capital city in Edom at one time. The conquering Messiah, approaching Jerusalem to reign after having avenged His people, is presented in imagery taken from the destruction of Edom, showing that He alone is "mighty to save."

3. ANGER . . . FURY . . . BLOOD: The Savior explains that the red coloring of His clothing is the result of His judgment against Israel's enemies. The splatter and stains from the "winepress" are, in reality, blood from those He has destroyed in His wrath. The apostle John alludes to verses 1–3 in describing the Second Coming of Christ, the Warrior-King (see Revelation 19:13, 15).

4. YEAR OF MY REDEEMED: The Messiah's future reckoning with the wicked will coincide with His redemption of Israel.

5. MY OWN ARM: The future salvation of Israel will be a singlehanded accomplishment of the Lord.

7. THE LOVINGKINDNESSES OF THE LORD: The prayer from Isaiah that follows (through Isiah 64:12) reviews God's compassionate acts toward His people in spite of their unfaithfulness to Him. The multiplied plurals in the opening verse imply that language is inadequate to recite all the goodness and undeserved mercies God has showered on the nation time after time because of His everlasting covenant with them. By His elective choice, they became His people and He their Savior. This alone guarantees that they will not always be false ("lie," verse 8), but someday true and faithful to God.

9. ANGEL OF HIS PRESENCE: This angel, who delivered the Israelites from Egypt, was none other than the Lord Himself. He is sometimes identified as the Angel of the Lord. He was close enough to His people that He felt their afflictions as if they were His own.

10. REBELLED AND GRIEVED HIS HOLY SPIRIT: In spite of the Lord's loving choice of and sympathy toward them, Israel continually turned their backs on God and spurned His lovingkindness toward them. Importantly, here is an illustration that the Holy Spirit is a person, since only a person can be grieved.

11. HE REMEMBERED . . . MIGHT NOT STUMBLE: The Lord, in spite of His people's perversity, neither forgot nor forsook His covenant with them. In contrasting their present state of destitution with that of blessing experienced by Moses' generation, the people of Israel lamented the loss of God's mighty works on their behalf and pleaded with the Lord that He would not forsake them.

14. MAKE YOURSELF A GLORIOUS NAME: The Lord's purpose for Israel was and is to make them great in order to magnify His name in the world.

15. WHERE ARE . . . YOUR MERCIES TOWARD ME?: On behalf of the people, Isaiah prays for new mercies for Israel such as God had exhibited toward them in the past.

16. ABRAHAM . . . ISRAEL: The nation's physical ancestors, Abraham and Jacob (Israel), played a crucial role in Jewish thinking. It had been the besetting temptation and sin of the Jews to rest on the mere privilege of descent from Abraham and Jacob (see Matthew 3:9; John 4:12; 8:39), but at last they renounce that mindset to trust God alone as Father.

17. MADE US STRAY . . . HARDENED OUR HEART: The sense is that God allowed the Israelites to stray and be burdened in their hearts. They were not denying their own guilt, but confessing that because of it, God gave them up to the consequences of their iniquitous choices.

18. TRODDEN DOWN YOUR SANCTUARY: The Babylonians, among others, had possessed the land given to Israel and desecrated God's sanctuary.

19. NEVER . . . NEVER: Israel's complaint was that her desolate condition was comparable to that of nations who had no unique relationship with the Lord.

A PLEA FOR HELP: Isaiah continues his prayer to God, pleading for the Lord to demonstrate His power toward Israel as He did in earlier days.

64:1. REND THE HEAVENS: Israel's response to her own complaint was a plea that God would burst forth to execute vengeance suddenly on His people's foes, manifesting Himself in judgment again as He did at Mt. Sinai (see Exodus 19:18). As God's name is to receive glory through His redemption of Israel, it also is to have widespread recognition because of His judgment against Israel's enemies.

3. AWESOME THINGS: Another reference to God's acts at Sinai.

4. THE EAR . . . THE EYE: God's judgmental manifestations are unique. No one has witnessed the likes of His awesome works on behalf of His own. Paul later adapted words from this verse to speak of direct revelation of God, imparted to His apostles and prophets, pertaining to mysteries hidden from mankind before the birth of the church (see 1 Corinthians 2:9).

5. WE NEED TO BE SAVED: Direct exposure to the awesome character of God's judgment brings a realization of sinners' need of salvation.

6. UNCLEAN THING . . . FILTHY RAGS: As in Isaiah 53:6, the prophet includes himself among those confessing their unworthiness to be in God's presence. He employs here the imagery of menstrual cloths used during a woman's period to picture uncleanness (see Leviticus 15:19–24). This is the proper understanding of even the best unbelievers' best actions.

7. NO ONE WHO CALLS ON YOUR NAME: The prophet finds no exception among a people whose iniquities had separated them from God. Such seeking and calling on the Lord, as Isaiah describes in 55:6–7, cannot occur apart from the powerful conviction and awakening of the sinful heart by the Holy Spirit.

Thus, Isaiah in his prayer recognizes God as a potter in control of clay (see 45:9–10) and pleads for Him to do a saving work (see 64:8). Such a work is what God promised to end His fury (see 54:7–8) and His memory of sin (see 64:9; 43:25).

11. BURNED UP WITH FIRE . . . LAID WASTE: Isaiah uttered these words many years before the fall of Jerusalem and the destruction of the Temple in 586 BC. Yet he laments over the state as though its downfall had already occurred. God's people were in desperate straits, and their prayers were urgent and persistent: "How can You stand by when Your people and Your land are so barren?"

Read Isaiah 66:1–24, noting the key words and phrases indicated below.

> GOD'S DWELLING: *Isaiah begins the final summary of his prophecy with a reminder that God is not looking for a temple of stone, since as Creator of all, the whole universe is His in which to dwell. Rather, He seeks a right heart.*

1. WHERE IS THE HOUSE THAT YOU WILL BUILD ME?: Stephen cited this passage before the Sanhedrin to point out their error in limiting God to a temple made with hands (see Acts 7:49–50). On the contrary, God is looking for a tender heart in which to dwell, one concerned with more than the mere externals of religion.

2. ON THIS ONE WILL I LOOK: Proud idolaters will be rejected and judged severely, but those who humbly and with a contrite heart obey God's Word will receive God's blessing and favor.

3. AS IF HE SLAYS A MAN: God loathes even the sacrifices of the wicked. They often killed children to offer in sacrifice (see Ezekiel 23:39). Some of the Jews were offering bulls as sacrifices with the same emptiness in their hearts as the pagans offering "a man" on the altar.

BREAKS A DOG'S NECK: This refers to offering dogs in sacrifice, which, as unclean animals, are associated with swine. To sacrifice a lamb with an attitude no different than if it were a dog betrayed the empty-heartedness of the offeror. All of these images are meant to illustrate the shallow hypocrisy of a person who makes an offering to God, but with no more heartbrokenness than a pagan who kills a child, offers a dog, sacrifices pig's blood, blesses an idol, and loves such abominations. God will judge all such actions.

5. YOUR BRETHREN WHO HATED YOU: The apostate Israelites intensified their rivalry with the faithful remnant and blasphemously said, "Let the LORD be glorified," in a sarcastic spirit (see Isaiah 5:19). In the end, "they shall be ashamed" because God's judgment will fall.

7–9. SHE WAS IN LABOR: Another comparison with the human birth process, intended this time to teach two lessons: (1) no birth can come until labor pains have occurred, and (2) when labor occurs, birth will surely follow. The point is that Israel's suffering will end with a delivery; the Lord will not impose travail on the remnant without bringing them to the kingdom.

11. FEED AND BE SATISFIED: The prophet compares Jerusalem to a nursing mother.

12. PEACE . . . LIKE A RIVER: The picture is of abundant peace, like that of a tranquil stream, a wadi filled with never-ending water that pictures the millennial wealth and prosperity of Israel.

14. SHALL BE KNOWN TO HIS SERVANTS: Prosperity will belong to the faithful remnant, but wrath to those who oppose the Lord.

15. WHIRLWIND . . . FLAMES OF FIRE: That the wrath of God will come to the rebels is expressed in language describing the end-time judgment.

16. THE SLAIN OF THE LORD SHALL BE MANY: The many who fight against the Lord when He comes to establish His kingdom will die (see Revelation 19:21).

17. SANCTIFY THEMSELVES AND PURIFY THEMSELVES: Sanctification and purification rites, when done for purposes of idol worship, will draw judgment from the one true God.

18. THEIR WORKS AND THEIR THOUGHTS: The Lord was aware of the motivations behind the actions of apostate Israelites.

19. THOSE . . . WHO ESCAPE: The faithful remnant of Israel is in view, who escape both the persecutions of their enemies and the judgment of God against those enemies.

TARSHISH AND PUL AND LUD . . . TUBAL AND JAVAN: Tarshish was possibly in Spain, Pul and Lud in North Africa, Tubal in northeast Asia Minor, and Javan in Greece. These represent Gentile populations that will hear of God's glory through the faithful remnant.

20. BRING ALL YOUR BRETHREN: As their offering to the Lord, the Gentiles who hear of God's glory will expedite the return of Israel's faithful remnant.

21. PRIESTS AND LEVITES: Some of the returning remnant will function in these specialized roles in the services of the millennial temple and memorial sacrifices.

22. YOUR DESCENDANTS AND YOUR NAME REMAIN: National Israel will have a never-ending existence through the Millennium and on into the new heavens and the new earth.

23. ALL FLESH SHALL COME TO WORSHIP BEFORE ME: All humanity will participate in worshiping the Lord at stipulated times during the temporal phase of the messianic kingdom.

24. WORM DOES NOT DIE . . . FIRE IS NOT QUENCHED: The corpses of those enduring everlasting torment will serve as a vivid reminder to all of the grievous nature and terrible consequences of rebellion against God. In referring to this verse, Jesus spoke of the Valley of Hinnom (see Mark 9:47–48).

UNLEASHING THE TEXT

1) What does Isaiah 58 say should be the intent of our hearts when we follow God's laws?

_____

_____

_____

_____

_____

2) How do the opening verses of Isaiah 61 point to the life and ministry of Jesus?

_____

_____

_____

3) When have you received help from God?

_____

_____

_____

_____

4) What was the primary theme of Isaiah 66, the final chapter in Isaiah's prophecy?

_____

_____

_____

_____

_____

EXPLORING THE MEANING

God values rightousness more than religious rituals. At the beginning of Isaiah 58, God highlights the hypocrisy of the leaders in Judah. These leaders wanted to know why God wasn't responding to their religious rituals: "'Why have we fasted,' they say, 'and You have not seen? Why have we afflicted our souls, and You take no notice?'" (verse 3).

The practices of fasting, offering sacrifices, and celebrating festivals were core elements of the Jewish people's outward religious practice. The residents of Judah had followed those practices, yet they still faced the threat of Assyria and other nations. They wanted to know why God hadn't honored their worship.

Having highlighted their questions, God provides His answer: "Is this not the fast that I have chosen: to loose the bonds of wickedness, to undo the heavy burdens, to let the oppressed go free, and that you break every yoke? Is it not to share your bread with the hungry, and that you bring to your house the poor who are cast out; when you see the naked, that you cover him, and not hide yourself from your own flesh?" (verses 6–7).

God had no interest in responding to the empty religious rituals of His people. He wanted them to act out their faith through love, justice, mercy, and compassion. He still does! The apostle James made that clear many centuries after Isaiah's ministry: "If anyone among you thinks he is religious, and does not bridle his tongue but deceives his own heart, this one's religion is useless. Pure and undefiled religion before God and the Father is this: to visit orphans and widows in their trouble, and to keep oneself unspotted from the world" (James 1:26–27). God is not impressed with false piety and empty rituals. As He told Samuel, "The LORD does not see as man sees; for man looks at the outward appearance, but the LORD looks at the heart" (1 Samuel 16:7).

Jesus is the ultimate fulfillment of Isaiah's prophecy. At the beginning of Jesus' public ministry, we read in the Gospels that He returned to His hometown of Nazareth. On the Sabbath, He took His place in the synagogue, according to His custom, and opened the scroll containing the prophecy from Isaiah. Here is what He read from Isaiah 61:1–2:

> The Spirit of the LORD is upon Me,
> Because He has anointed Me
> To preach the gospel to the poor;
> He has sent Me to heal the brokenhearted,
> To proclaim liberty to the captives
> And recovery of sight to the blind,
> To set at liberty those who are oppressed;
> To proclaim the acceptable year of the LORD (Luke 4:18–19).

When Jesus had finished reading, He made a statement that was both incredible and incredibly profound: "Today this Scripture is fulfilled in your hearing" (verse 21). Jesus was fully aware that Isaiah's prophecy, and these verses specifically, was focused on the Messiah. As such, Jesus allowed no doubts among His hearers. *He* was the Messiah, and *He* was publicly stepping into that role in order to begin the mission God had sent Him to complete.

As a side note, it is critical for Christians to remember that Jesus' mission continues to this day. As those who have been transformed by His atoning work and indwelt by the Holy Spirit, we have been set aside for the work of the gospel. It's our privilege to bring the light of God's Word to those still spiritually blind—to call those still held captive by sin to the freedom found only in knowing and loving Christ.

We should approach God with humility. In contrast to the leadership of Judah, who demanded to know why God did not honor their religious fasts and sacrifices, Isaiah offered a prayer of his own—a plea for God's help. One of the most striking elements of that prayer is the level of humility that Isaiah displayed before God.

Isaiah begins this prayer in chapter 63, beginning in verse 7, by recognizing God's compassion in spite of Israel's unfaithfulness, followed by a repentant plea to return to a right relationship with Him. Chapter 64 continues the prayer with several verses expressing a desire to see God burst onto the world in power, just as He had done in earlier generations. But Isaiah then quickly confesses the shortcomings of his people: "You are indeed angry, for we have sinned—in these ways we continue; and we need to be saved" (verse 5). Isaiah follows that confession with this statement about the corruption of sin: "We are all like an unclean thing, and all our righteousnesses are like filthy rags" (verse 6). He concludes with an acknowledgment of God's control over all things, including humanity: "But now, O LORD, You are our Father; we are the clay, and You our potter; and all we are the work of Your hand" (verse 8).

It's easy for us to fall into the trap of self-righteousness. We often believe, because of the comfort and relative affluence of our modern lives, that we are experiencing God's blessings as a result of our own goodness—our own worthiness. In truth, we would do well to remember Isaiah's humility as we confess before, serve, worship, pray, and follow our holy God.

REFLECTING ON THE TEXT

5) Where does empty ritualism show up in the church today? Why is it offensive to God?

_____

_____

_____

_____

_____

_____

6) In what ways are you tempted to "go through the motions" in corporate worship, and in your private devotion to God? How do you guard against such hypocrisy?

_____

_____

_____

_____

_____

_____

7) What does it mean to be "covered with the robe of righteousness" (Isaiah 61:10)?

_____

_____

_____

_____

_____

8) On a practical level, what does it look like to demonstrate humility before God?

_____

_____

_____

_____

_____

PERSONAL RESPONSE

9) What can you do this week to simply enjoy time in God's presence?

_____

_____

_____

_____

_____

10) Where are you in danger of a self-righteous or arrogant attitude?

_____

_____

_____

_____

_____

12

REVIEWING KEY PRINCIPLES

DRAWING NEAR
What has Isaiah's prophecy taught you about the Person and work of Christ?

_____

_____

_____

_____

_____

_____

_____

_____

THE CONTEXT
The book of Isaiah is one of the longest in Scripture. It represents an enormous collection of rich and varied themes, promises, prophecies, and judgments. In the end, however, what God communicated through Isaiah, His prophet, is perhaps best summed up in the meaning of the prophet's name: "The Lord is salvation."

The people of Isaiah's day still paid lip service to God—they went through the motions of their religious rituals, but their hearts were far from Him. Others had fully succumbed to the influence of idolatry, forsaking God altogether. They feared the punishment their sin deserved—punishment that, as Isaiah prophesied, would be poured out over generations, culminating in the exile of Babylonian captivity.

But the emphasis of Isaiah's prophecy isn't merely the coming judgment—it's that the Lord is unceasingly faithful to His people, and that He would redeem and restore them in spite of their sinfulness. In Isaiah's immediate context, that meant the Lord would preserve them from the Assyrian assault. But God's words through the prophet also pointed ahead to the restoration of His people after the Babylonian exile. Most importantly, God uses Isaiah to point ahead to the coming Messiah, providing copious, specific details that would all be fulfilled in the Person and work of Christ. Although Isaiah was writing seven centuries before the birth of Christ, we become intimately aquainted with the Lord in His incarnation, and look forward to the atonement only He could provide to redeem His people.

Some of Isaiah's prophecy still remains unfulfilled, as he points ahead to the New Jerusalem and the reconstitution of God's covenant people. But even in looking forward to the end of history, the redemptive theme of the book remains in focus. The glories that await further emphasize the grace, mercy, and faithfulness of the Lord. Such eternal blessings and benefits are only available through the atoning work of His Son and the transforming work of His Spirit. Our God is a saving God, and He alone can rescue and redeem His people from the due penalty of their sins. He is faithful, even when we are not.

EXPLORING THE MEANING

Serving God is an awesome responsibility. In Isaiah 6, the prophet recalls the moment when God appeared to him in a vision called him into His service. "I heard the voice of the Lord, saying: 'Whom shall I send, and who will go for Us?'" Many readers of the Bible are inspired by Isaiah's quick response: "Here am I! Send me'" (verse 8).

However, it's important not to miss Isaiah's earlier interaction with God at the beginning of the chapter. After the death of King Uzziah, Isaiah supernaturally witnessed a vision of God's heavenly throne room. The sight was both awesome and terrible, causing Isaiah to cry out, "Woe is me, for I am undone! Because I am a man of unclean lips, and I dwell in the midst of a people of unclean lips; for my eyes have seen the King, the LORD of hosts" (verse 5).

Isaiah's cry mirrors Peter's after he recognized Jesus as the Messiah and exclaimed, "Depart from me, for I am a sinful man, O Lord!" (Luke 5:8). In fact, throughout the Bible, people almost unanimously fall to the ground and worship in fear whenever they come into God's presence. Those of us who serve as disciples of Jesus today will do well to remember that our Savior is also the supreme Lord and Judge of the universe. Our service to Him is not a casual commitment but rather an awesome responsibility.

Biblical prophecy typically involves layers. The Old Testament contains many passages that point forward to the life and ministry of Jesus. But few are better known than Isaiah 9:6–7:

> For unto us a Child is born,
> Unto us a Son is given;
> And the government will be upon His shoulder.
> And His name will be called
> Wonderful, Counselor, Mighty God,
> Everlasting Father, Prince of Peace.
> Of the increase of His government and peace
> There will be no end,
> Upon the throne of David and over His kingdom,
> To order it and establish it with judgment and justice
> From that time forward, even forever.
> The zeal of the LORD of hosts will perform this.

Reading these verses, it's clear that many aspects of this Messianic prophecy have already been fulfilled by Christ. The phrase "unto us a Child is born," for example, points back to Jesus' miraculous birth, which Isaiah had already promised in chapter 7. In addition, Jesus was demonstrably a descendent of David (see Matthew 1:1–17), and throughout the New Testament the authors affirmed Him to be "Mighty God."

However, several aspects of Isaiah's prophecy are yet to be fulfilled. For instance, we know from Scripture that Jesus will one day take the government upon His shoulders (see Revelation 2:27; 19:15). However, we are also painfully aware that this has not yet taken place. Similarly, Jesus has not yet brought "peace" to the world, nor has He established His perfect "justice." Those promises will be fulfilled at the end of history.

These verses shine a light on the complexity of biblical prophecy and the need for careful, objective interpretation. The people of Jesus' day were fixated on the temporal fulfillment of Isaiah's prophecies and longed for a leader to free them from Rome's oppressive rulers. Therefore, they sought only a Messiah who would take the reins of David's throne as a military King. Their skewed view of Isaiah's prophecies ultimately led them to reject Christ as their true Messiah and cry out for His execution (see Matthew 27:22). Your priorities and timetables likewise won't always match up with God's, and you shouldn't expect all His promises and blessings to arrive according to your schedule.

God is Judge over all evil. Not only does God exercise His authority to judge evil nations and kings, but He also judges evil in every instance and from every source—including Satan himself. In Isaiah 14, the prophet was describing the future fall of the king of Babylon when he suddenly made this statement: "How you are fallen from heaven, O Lucifer, son of the morning! How you are cut down to the ground, you who weakened the nations! For you have said in your heart: 'I will ascend into heaven, I will exalt my throne above the stars of God . . . I will be like the Most High'" (verses 12–14).

Many see in Isaiah's words a twofold denunciation. The prophet was still speaking of the humiliation and defeat awaiting Babylon's king. Yet he also was making a distinct connection between that king and Satan—the evil power behind the scenes. He is the "prince of the power of the air" (Ephesians 2:2) and "the great dragon . . . who deceives the whole world" (Revelation 12:9). Isaiah showed that Babylon's evil was directly connected to Satan and was a reflection of his ongoing rebellion against God.

Of course, the wonderful news is that Satan is a *defeated* foe. Neither he nor evil will win the day in the end because Jesus has already won the victory through His death and resurrection on the cross. As John declared, "I heard a loud voice saying in heaven, 'Now salvation, and strength, and the kingdom of our God, and the power of His Christ have come, for the accuser of our brethren, who accused them before our God day and night, has been cast down. And they overcame him by the blood of the Lamb and by the word of their testimony, and they did not love their lives to the death'" (Revelation 12:10–11).

God goes to great lengths to speak with humanity. There is a moment in Isaiah 20 that can come across as genuinely surprising—perhaps even shocking—to modern readers. As the prophet writes, "At the same time the LORD spoke by Isaiah the son of Amoz, saying, 'Go, and remove the sackcloth from your body, and take your sandals off your feet.' And he did so, walking naked and barefoot" (verse 2). Isaiah was commanded to walk around naked *for three years* to illustrate the coming judgment against Egypt and Ethiopia, in which both countries would experience captivity and hardship for three years.

This might sound like an extreme way to make a point. Yet the reality is that throughout Scripture, God often uses extreme measures to get people's attention. For example, God commanded Hosea, another prophet, to marry an unfaithful woman as an illustration of Israel's spiritual adultery (see Hosea 1:2). He commanded the prophet Ezekiel to lie on his side for 390 days and eat bread baked over cow dung to warn the nation of Israel about God's coming judgment. He commanded Jeremiah to buy a field when his country was overrun by Babylonian invaders and everyone else was converting their land into cash and valuables.

Of course, the most striking method God has used to capture the attention of humanity was the Incarnation—including the birth, life, ministry, death, and resurrection of Jesus Christ. As John writes, "The Word became flesh and dwelt among us" (John 1:14). Through Jesus, God took on human nature and a body of flesh to offer Himself as a perfect sacrifice so that the penalty for our sins could be paid and our relationship with God could be restored.

This world is not our home. One of the themes emphasized throughout Isaiah's prophecy is the coming Day of the Lord, when God's judgment will fully fall upon the earth and its inhabitants. Part of that judgment will include the destruction of our planet. In Isaiah's words:

> The earth is violently broken,
> The earth is split open,
> The earth is shaken exceedingly.
> The earth shall reel to and fro like a drunkard,
> And shall totter like a hut;
> Its transgression shall be heavy upon it,
> And it will fall, and not rise again (24:19–20).

As we've seen, the Day of the Lord is a theme revisited many times throughout Scripture. For instance, the prophet Joel wrote, "The sun shall be turned into darkness, and the moon into blood, before the coming of the great and awesome day of the LORD" (2:31). Peter added, "But the day of the Lord will come as a thief in the night, in which the heavens will pass away with a great noise, and the elements will melt with fervent heat; both the earth and the works that are in it will be burned up" (2 Peter 3:10).

Ultimately, however, this destruction will lay the groundwork for something wonderful: a new earth devoid of the corruption of sin. This world is not our home; it is a stopping place. Our actual home will be an eternal paradise. John received a vision of this new home, which caused him to write these words to the church: "I saw a new heaven and a new earth, for the first heaven and the first earth had passed away. . . . [There] God will wipe away every tear from their eyes; there shall be no more death, nor sorrow, nor crying. There shall be no more pain, for the former things have passed away" (Revelation 21:1, 4).

Jesus is our Cornerstone. Most of the prophets included strong imagery and visual language in their prophecies, and Isaiah was no exception. In fact, many of the most famous passages recorded in his book are centered on key images. We find one such image in Isaiah 28:16: "Therefore thus says the Lord GOD: 'Behold, I lay in Zion a stone for a foundation, a tried stone, a precious cornerstone, a sure foundation; whoever believes will not act hastily.'"

The image of a cornerstone would have been clear for the people of Isaiah's day. Buildings in that time were generally constructed on top of a stone foundation—with the cornerstone serving as the first and most important piece. Every other stone in that foundation would be laid to match and support the cornerstone. Therefore, if the cornerstone were faulty or set improperly, the entire building would be suspect.

By using that analogy, Isaiah was creating a contrast between the kings and leaders of his day and the future Messiah. The current kings of Israel and Judah were fickle and unreliable—flawed and faulty cornerstones. In the future, however, God would send His Messiah to serve as a sure and certain foundation for His people and His kingdom.

Jesus revealed that He Himself is the cornerstone (see Mark 12:10), and the New Testament consistently affirms that this imagery pointed to Christ as the foundation of the church. Paul wrote, "Now, therefore, you are no longer strangers and foreigners, but fellow citizens with the saints and members of the household of God, having been built on the foundation of the apostles and prophets, Jesus Christ Himself being the chief cornerstone, in whom the whole building, being fitted together, grows into a holy temple in the Lord" (Ephesians 2:19–21). The apostle Peter also referenced Isaiah's cornerstone in his first epistle (see 1 Peter 2:6).

The best prayers are honest prayers. Hezekiah was the king of Judah during this time of attack from Assyria, and he is notable among Judah's kings as someone who understood the value of prayer. When Sennacherib had to withdraw from Jerusalem to deal with other attackers, he sent a letter to Hezekiah promising to return and finish his intended conquest. That turned out to be an empty threat, but no one knew it at the time.

For that reason, it's important to note what Hezekiah did in response. First, he went up to the temple and spread out the letter before God. Then he prayed: "O LORD of hosts, God of Israel, the One who dwells between the cherubim, You are God, You alone, of all the kingdoms of the earth. You have made heaven and earth. Incline Your ear, O Lord, and hear; open Your eyes, O Lord, and see; and hear all the words of Sennacherib, which he has sent to reproach the living God" (Isaiah 37:16–17). Hezekiah asked God to save the people of Judah so "all the kingdoms of the earth may know that You are the LORD, You alone" (verse 20).

At another time during his reign, Hezekiah had experienced a profound sickness. God told Isaiah to give Hezekiah the news that that sickness would be fatal. Here is how the king responded: "Hezekiah turned his face toward the wall, and prayed to the LORD, and said, 'Remember now, O LORD, I pray, how I have walked before You in truth and with a loyal heart, and have done what is good in Your sight.' And Hezekiah wept bitterly" (38:2–3).

In both instances, Hezekiah's prayers were an honest reflection of his troubled heart. He was bitterly disappointed at the thought of his coming death, so he expressed those emotions honestly before God, even to the point of weeping. (Interestingly, God responded to Hezekiah's prayer by granting him fifteen more years of life.) He knew he could not defeat Sennacherib and the armies of Assyria, so he asked God to save his people. The point is this: Our best prayers are those moments when we take God as His Word and speak with Him honestly from our hearts.

Idolatry is foolishness. Idolatry was one of the key reasons God's people in Israel and Judah had wandered away from their special relationship to Him. There are many reasons why the Israelites were enticed by the false gods of the surrounding nations. For one thing, many cults used temple prostitutes as part of their "worship" experiences. For another, worshiping idols gave people a sense of comfort and control. It was much more convenient to fashion an idol and make sacrifices in your home, rather than submit yourself to the Creator of the universe.

Isaiah addressed the topic of idolatry from several different angles. In one humorous passage, he describes the foolishness of people's burning one end of a log to provide warmth and to cook their food, and then fashioning the other end into an idol to be worshiped: "And the rest of it he makes into a god, his carved image. He falls down before it and worships it, prays to it and says, 'Deliver me, for you are my god!'" (44:17). Isaiah also declared, "Those who make an image, all of them are useless, and their precious things shall not profit; they are their own witnesses; they neither see nor know, that they may be ashamed" (verse 9).

These references to idols seem archaic, but the truth is that idolatry is not a thing of the past. Rather, idolatry is fully practiced in the modern world—including by those who call themselves Christians. An idol is anything we allow to occupy God's rightful place in our lives. It's anything we worship other than God. Money qualifies as an idol for many people in our culture. So does power, pleasure, entertainment, and comfort. We no longer create carven images in most of the modern world. Yet we often still seek to replace God with items or goals that have no capacity to save, bless, or provide what we truly need.

UNLEASHING THE TEXT

1) What encourages you about the way God has fulfilled Isaiah's prophecies? Which as-yet unfulfilled prophecies provide similar comfort and assurance?

_____

_____

_____

_____

_____

_____

_____

2) What are some unanswered questions you will pursue further after completing this study?

_____

_____

_____

_____

_____

_____

3) How has studying the book of Isaiah added to your understanding of Jesus?

_____

_____

_____

_____

_____

4) Why is it critical for us to understand that God is aware of our lives and cares about us on a personal level?

_____

_____

_____

_____

_____

PERSONAL RESPONSE

5) Why was the atoning work of Christ—described in Isaiah's prophecies—necessary for the redemption of God's people? Explain.

_____

_____

_____

_____

6) In what areas of your life have you been most convicted during this study? What exact things will you do to address these convictions? Be specific.

_____

_____

_____

_____

_____

_____

_____

_____

7) What have you learned about God's nature and character throughout this study? How should that knowledge affect your everyday life?

_____

_____

_____

_____

_____

_____

_____

8) In what areas do you hope to grow spiritually over the coming weeks and months? What can you do to support and stimulate that growth?

_____

_____

_____

_____

_____

_____

If you would like to continue in your study of the Old Testament, read the next title in this series: *Jeremiah & Lamentations: Judgment and Grace.*

Also Available in the John MacArthur Bible Study Series

The MacArthur Bible Studies provide intriguing examinations of the whole of Scripture. Each of the 35 guides (16 Old Testament and 19 New Testament) incorporates extensive commentary, detailed observations on overriding themes, and probing questions to help you study the Word of God.

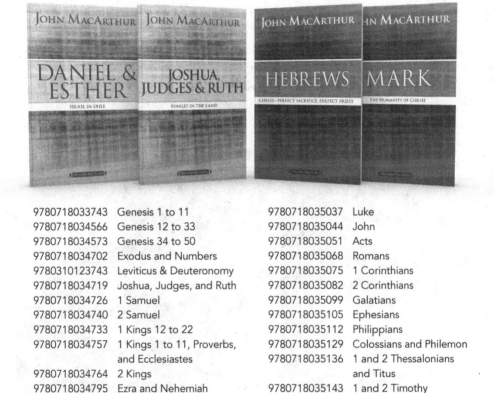

Available now at your favorite bookstore.
More volumes coming soon.

THOMAS NELSON
Since 1798

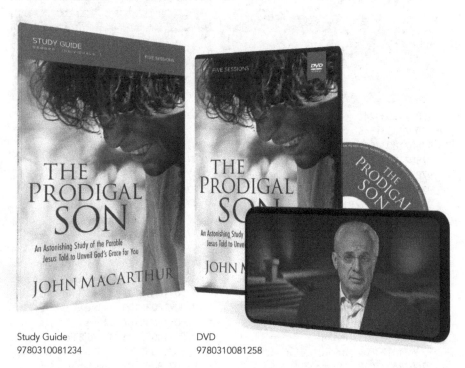

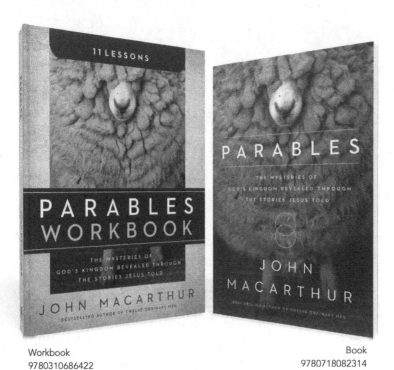